"If you remain unconvinced that from our deepest
wounds springs our brightest light and transcenden
words of Janina Scarlet. For those who've lost faith
is truly possible, *Super-Women* will restore you, persuade you the work is worth it, and show you the way to home. Innovative, inclusive, and expansive—this book is for ALL women!"

—**Erica Mather,** yoga therapist and author of *Your Body, Your Best Friend*

"In her therapy workbook, *Super-Women,* psychologist Janina Scarlet leads her reader through a journey of virtual group therapy to create the emotional safety and connection they need to thrive. In it, Scarlet presents a vibrant and diverse cast of female characters whose own healing experiences support the reader's healing from chronic shame, trauma, and disconnection. Framing pain and vulnerability as portals to compassion and strength—and ultimately their own 'superhero' story—Scarlet has masterfully integrated the most advanced narrative and cognitive behavioral techniques available. "

—**Aprilia West, PsyD, MT,** psychologist, executive leadership coach, author of *What You Feel Is Not All There Is,* and coauthor of *Emotion Efficacy Therapy*

"*Super-Women* by Janina Scarlet is the book you didn't know you needed—but you do. This book lets women know that *it is* okay to have emotional needs. I love that this book integrates diverse voices, amplifies women's experience, and addresses the context in which women live today. Janina's calm and steady voice invites you into a sanctuary where you can put down—for a moment—your arms, your masks, and just be. And in this stillness, you can find your strengths. I highly recommend it!"

—**Lisa Coyne, PhD,** founder and director of New England Center for OCD and Anxiety, assistant professor at Harvard Medical School, and coauthor of *Stuff That's Loud*

"*Super-Women* by Janina Scarlet walks women through a healing journey from building emotional safety to cultivating compassion. This ACT-based self-help book is a must-have for women struggling with the pain of trauma and other emotional challenges in their lives. I will be recommending it to my women clients. It will support them to not simply recover, but to fully engage in growth and meaning as they step forward into values-based living."

—**Robyn D. Walser, PhD,** licensed clinical psychologist, author of *The Heart of ACT,* and coauthor of *Learning ACT* and *The Mindful Couple*

"Janina Scarlet's compassion, courage, skillfulness, abundant wisdom, and expertise shine through in *Super-Women.* Through many super-women sharing both their own personal experiences and their experiences of applying the skills necessary to become a superhero in real life, you too will get the opportunity to experience emotional safety and connection to give you the courage, compassion, and skills to become a superhero yourself in the face of the anxieties and traumas you have faced as a woman."

—**Aisling Leonard-Curtin,** chartered psychologist with the Psychological Society of Ireland, peer-reviewed acceptance and commitment therapy (ACT) trainer, codirector of ACT Now Purposeful Living, and coauthor of *The Power of Small*

"When I finished reading *Super-Women,* I immediately texted Janina to share my appreciation and excitement for this manuscript. It is beautifully narrated, illustrated, and it does an incredible job blending ACT skills throughout every single page. This self-help book is a resourceful guide for readers on how to shift from painful experiences into personal moments of growth, purpose, and meaning. I hope every reader finds their superhero within!"

—**Patricia E. Zurita Ona, PsyD,** author of *Living Beyond OCD Using Acceptance and Commitment Therapy* and *The ACT Workbook for Teens with OCD*

"Janina Scarlet has provided a map for the journey to discovering your inner superheroine. With compassionate courage and wisdom, this book will help you navigate the challenges of trauma, anxiety, and depression. Filled with helpful exercises and real-world examples, this book will be an indispensable companion for you as you join the ranks of real-life super-women that have faced dragons and unleashed their power into the world."

—**Laura Silberstein-Tirch, PsyD,** founding director of The Center for Compassion Focused Therapy, and author of *How to Be Nice to Yourself*

SUPERHERO THERAPY *for* WOMEN BATTLING ANXIETY, DEPRESSION & TRAUMA

JANINA SCARLET, PHD

New Harbinger Publications, Inc.

Publisher's Note

Distributed in Canada by Raincoast Books

First published in Great Britain in 2020 by Robinson

New Harbinger Publications, Inc.
5674 Shattuck Avenue
Oakland, CA 94609
www.newharbinger.com

Cover design by Sara Christian

Acquired by Ryan Buresh

Printed in the United States of America

23 22 21

10 9 8 7 6 5 4 3 2 1 First Printing

To all the Super-Women who face their own dragons on a daily basis. You are my role models. Thank you for your courage. Thank you for being wonderful.

To be a woman

To be a woman means feeling not thin enough,
Lost in the distorted image of every mirror.
It's to be blamed about how your skirt
Or your tone caused the pain you endured
At the hand or the fists of someone
Who promised to never hurt you.
It means being told that sex is an obligation
To be had without any detestation.
It means being called "crazy"
For asking for fidelity
Or for having emotions
Such as insecurity or jealousy.
It means being praised for starvation,
Always anxious about a negative evaluation.
It means being a contradiction,
Self-evaluating like it's an addiction.
It means being an impossibility,
It means having a super ability
To be in multiple places and play multiple roles,
To face the world and the internet trolls.
And what it really means
Is the courage to meet our own needs,
To stand up after constant defeats.
It means to look in the mirror
And see the superhero,
The one that has been there
More times than you could be aware,
As your power shines through
Brighter than you ever knew.

Contents

Foreword

"Where are your feet?" Her voice was gentle and calm—but I looked up incredulously, perceiving this question as a jolting departure from the subject. Through hauntingly quiet tears, I had just resolutely told Janina that the pain was too much. That if brokenness could actually stop a heart from beating, I would be long gone. And I just wanted to die, so the pain would stop. Janina's face was open and gentle, full of compassion, yet unshaken. "I'm here, Chase," she said. "I'd like to ask you to put your hand on your heart and breathe with me." We did. "Now tell me, where are your feet?"

And so began the journey of my healing with the work of Dr. Janina Scarlet. By that chilly winter afternoon in 2016, Janina was already my colleague through Pop Culture Hero Coalition, which I founded in 2013 with author Carrie Goldman. Through the years, I had produced and moderated panels all over the country with Janina brilliantly teaching self-compassion and empowerment, based in her own journey from arriving in the United States as a child refugee and navigating unthinkable pain, to her earning two doctorates and becoming an acclaimed author, therapist, podcaster, and speaker. I had already volunteered my work with the Coalition for years because I saw firsthand that the healing Janina brought for countless people was real.

But deep down, I didn't dare believe or even dream that healing was also possible for me.

We are all too capable of jumping on the bandwagon of the wounding that the world does. As if the damage was not already enough, we bully ourselves and participate in our own destruction. After mistreatment, shame, and other forms of psychological abuse, I had bought in to the notion that I was not enough. I held onto the arrows—shot out of someone else's misplaced jealousy, ignorance, and fear—that pierced my sense of self. And like so many, following trauma, I turned on myself and used their critical voices as my own. Instead of recognizing the sad truths about those who hurt us, we turn our pain inward and end up feeling hopeless, bereft of possibility, without even oneself to call a friend. But being bullied or abused was never our fault. Those voices never spoke the truth about us. Not even close.

As girls and women, we have often been socialized to fit into a mold of others' needs and desires. After belittlement and rejection, our propensity to find our identity in others' harmful words and actions also causes us to repress our wise minds, our abilities, our talents and impulses. Those gems inside us, when cultivated with respect and care, have the potential to free and heal our lives, as well as powerfully impact the world.

In her powerful graphic novel, *Dark Agents*, Janina shows us the way to "Embrace the dark and guard the light," and what she has helped me understand is that we cannot escape pain by running from it or even by fighting it. As Carl Jung wisely said, whatever is not brought to light becomes our destiny. We walk into our futures by bravely processing our pasts, with the kind of tools and support Janina shows you here. And you can. Because, as you will see, you are a Super-Woman.

These words of Marianne Williamson's ring with truth: "Our deepest fear is not that we are inadequate. Our deepest fear is that we are powerful beyond measure. It is our light, not our darkness, that most frightens us. We ask ourselves, 'Who am I to be brilliant, gorgeous, talented, fabulous?' Actually, who are you not to be?" Let that sink in. "Your playing small doesn't serve the world. There's nothing enlightened about shrinking so that other people won't feel insecure around you," she continues. "And as we let our own light shine, we subconsciously give other people permission to do the same."

And as they say in AA, "Don't leave before the miracle happens." Somehow, I found my feet that afternoon (you'll understand, too, in chapter 3 on Building Emotional Safety), and I stayed. It's hard to say when things began to shift for me. There was no big aha or Damascus moment.

But with Janina's voice in my head and heart, the healing of my life began and continues to happen. As you will experience, Janina is an expert storyteller, and so a big part is asking myself, daily, "What do I want to be my story?" Or as Mary Oliver so enticingly asks, "Tell me, what is it you plan to do with your one wild and precious life?" I learned that healing takes place with a persistent contending for your life—some days actively moving forward, some days struggling with all your might to free yourself from the quicksand of trauma—but all of those days are fierce. And all of those days ask only one thing of us: that we do the next right thing.

Janina leads you through doing exactly that. And that is how you realize you are a Super-Woman.

For me, many of those quicksand days have been filled with still, silent tears, where the pain cuts too deep to even cry out. One dark day, I sat yet again at a friend's kitchen table, broken. Disintegrated. Telling her I felt like I was the consistency and worth of a piece of wet toilet paper on the floor. The words my friend Sandy spoke were the last ones on earth I thought I would hear. "You are going to get through this. And your healing will spread like wildfire."

As powerful as those words were, they felt like torment, a tease of better times that felt unattainable. Like an arrow piercing an already-open wound, even hope—no, especially hope—was excruciating, too ludicrous to even remotely consider. And even if it were true, I reasoned, I can't go through what it will take. It felt like taking the journey from here to there wouldn't be worth it, no matter how good it might be on the other side.

Spoiler: the journey is worth it.

Janina's work is what got me from there to here—one day of persistence and self-compassion at a time. Because of grief, and loss, and betrayal, life can still be unthinkably hard at times—but because I now have tools, my life has become unrecognizably good, joyful, and powerful, and so victoriously well-worth living.

With all our fears and the features we perceive as flaws, Janina invites each of us into our own journey to acknowledge that we are Super-Women. Armed with a shield of self-compassion and a sword of resilience, Janina stands with us as we put on the boots of persistence and a belt of healthy identity. With the nourishment of self-kindness and the tools of rigorous honesty, accountability, empathy, and purpose, she beacons us to join an army of Super-Women. An army of love.

Your journey with Janina will help you to discover your needs... starting with the realization that you get to have them.

"Where are your feet?" My hope is that, in applying the understandings and concepts in this book to your own life, you will find them resolutely facing and then walking away from invalidation, self-doubt, shame, neglect, blame, abuse, and other forms of violence and trauma. My hope is that you will find your feet rooted in support. Self-compassion. Self-kindness. Sisterhood. Resilience. Empathy. Strength.

And the overflowing joy that comes from leading others to do the same. And then? Yes. Your healing will spread like wildfire.

In unity,

—Chase Masterson
Founder & CEO, Pop Culture Hero Coalition
@SuperheroIRL

Chapter 1

Welcome to the Sanctuary

The world might sometimes feel too painful and too overwhelming to manage. Worse, sometimes we might be chastised for how much we struggle to cope with our challenges and triggers. We might seek a safe place, a place to talk about the pain we are feeling, a place in which we are allowed to be truly and fully ourselves. A place in which we can feel all of our emotions safely without being judged or being told that we are "too emotional" or "too sensitive."

This book is my attempt to create such a place for you. In this book you will be invited to join a metaphorical sanctuary, a place in which you may feel safe. Safe to be you, safe to talk about, process, and think about some of the painful experiences you may have had or are currently going through. Throughout the book, you will be invited to create your own sanctuary, join a metaphorical support group, and learn coping tools to help you during some of your painful experiences.

Some of the topics we will be working on may be triggering. An emotional trigger is a sudden change of emotion, such as anger, rage, fear, devastation, or other similar emotions, in a response to a particular situation, such as when someone is being critical or unkind. An emotional trigger is often (though not always) associated with a painful experience in our past. If you notice yourself feeling overwhelmed by any of the material you are reading about, it is perfectly okay to take a break and return when you are feeling ready. There is never any need to force yourself to push yourself beyond your means. This is your sanctuary. Your safe space. And the way that you interact with it is completely up to you. Your sanctuary is always here for you, and in it you are always accepted just the way you are and in any way you feel. As a part of this process, we will be working on acknowledging our origin stories and building on them to help you tap into your own superpowers, ones you may not have realized that you already have.

My own origin story began in Ukraine, where I was born and raised. After being exposed to Chernobyl radiation as a small child, my health suffered. I felt "weak" and "broken." Having spent a good portion of my childhood sick and in and out of hospitals, I dived into reading. Books became my closest friends, a sweet balm to support me in my loneliest times. Most books talked about amazing heroes—knights, princes, Musketeers—characters who went on amazing adventures, defeating evil villains and saving the day. I wanted to be like them. I wanted to join them, to fight the dragons alongside them. They possessed the kind of resilience I wanted to have. Their lives had meaning. They stood for something. However, all of my favorite characters were men. In all the books I read as a child, the men were the heroes and the women had only two passive roles: to be rescued and to be beautiful.

I remember dreaming of being able to bend the gender rules so that women could join the ranks of the Musketeers, solve crime alongside Sherlock Holmes, and fight the monsters, too. When I brought this idea to one of my elderly neighbors, she laughed.

"Girls don't fight," she said.

"Well, then maybe I don't want to be a girl!" I cried at her.

Upon hearing this, my grandfather, a Holocaust survivor, took it upon himself to become my feminist role model. He pulled me aside and told me that he had other books for me, only they were written in a secret invisible language. He would take out a blank piece of paper and would move his finger left to right as if reading some kind of invisible magic ink. He read the stories out loud, stories about a brave little girl, me, whose brother and male cousins were kidnapped by an evil monster. I was the only one who was able to find the monster and stop him before he ate the members of my family. Without ever making it obvious, my grandfather taught me that girls can be equal to boys and that girls can stand up to men when men are behaving badly.

I learned and continue to learn lessons about myself, about humanity, and about the beauty and dangers of this world. One of the most pertinent lessons I learned was when I was walking home one night. That night I walked home alone to the beat of the Beatles playing on my headphones. I did not notice the man creeping up behind me.

That night will forever be engraved into my memory because that was the night that I learned that walking by myself after dark was not safe. That was the night I learned to keep turning around to check my surroundings. A different incident taught me that it was not safe to go outside in the daylight when a man grabbed my arm and yelled at me for refusing to give him my phone number.

Years later, these "lessons" remain, with just a few minutes having changed the course of my life forever: a man walking behind me on a dimly or even a brightly lit street; a man approaching me to ask for time or directions; a male stranger showing up unannounced at my workplace to ask for my autograph. All bring an equal degree of fight-flight-and-freeze response to my body.

My story is not unique. Women and people of other genders may have been affected by some of the people in their lives who have contributed to their struggles. Many individuals across the world experience similar triggers in terms of feeling unsafe around certain people. They may feel uncomfortable when a person approaches them suddenly, makes certain remarks, comes up too close to them, or touches them without permission. Many of us have been taught to smile and to "not cause a scene" even as we might feel frozen with fear.

In October 2017, the #MeToo hashtag went viral. It removed the world's blindfold about individuals who experienced sexual harassment and assault—including people across all races, gender identities, and sexual orientations. That year, the world saw the survivors, the heroes from around the world. The world saw their faces and learned their names. Heroes are people who stand for what they believe in, and superheroes are heroes with remarkable abilities. Superheroes are people like you who may struggle with physical or emotional pain, people like you who have exhibited tremendous courage in facing their fears, people like you who have already done the unexpected and the impossible.

> My biological father, an alcoholic, abandoned us when I was a baby and threatened to kill my mother and me.
>
> I think I've always had anxiety, but I never understood what it was until I was an adult. After my assault, I suffered serious depression during my first year away at college. I didn't tell anyone about what had happened. I internalized the shame and humiliation and powerlessness.
>
> Since then, I have taken medication and gone to therapy to help manage the symptoms, and I have zero shame about that. I've also found writing to be cathartic. I don't always journal about personal experiences; sometimes I write creative stories or fan fiction and it's through another character dealing with an issue that I find inspiration and relief.
>
> Don't give up on yourself, no matter what. You are worth the time and the energy it takes to get better or get through whatever you are struggling with. Showing yourself love is not selfish, it's necessary. Trust me, you're worth it.
>
> —Tanya

As you continue your journey throughout this book, feel free to take as much time as you need. Give yourself permission to practice or not practice any of the exercises outlined here, and to review or skip any of the readings. This book is a safe space in which you are always welcome. It is a place in which you are allowed, and all your emotions, thoughts, and reactions are understandable and supported. This space is here for you to utilize at any time and in any way you wish.

Creating emotional safety for yourself

Psychologists Kristin Neff and Chris Germer talk about the importance of creating psychological safety through *opening* and *closing*.[1] Opening refers to the willingness to receive or connect with something or someone. In this case, opening would mean the willingness to read the material presented in this book and to practice the skills outlined here. When we are open, we are able to receive new information and are able to connect with vulnerable parts of ourselves.

However, sometimes we need to close. This means that sometimes we may feel triggered, overwhelmed, reminded of something excruciating... and thus, some things might be too painful to read or connect with. That is absolutely okay and it may mean that we may need to close. Closing in this case may mean taking a breathing break, allowing ourselves to disconnect from the painful material, and return whenever it feels safe to do so.

This book is your sanctuary. There is no need for striving, forcing, or pushing yourself. You already have enough of that going on. So, as you are going through this book, give yourself permission to go at your own speed and to notice any striving or shaming that might come up for you. Oftentimes, we are so used to doing things we believe we *should* do that we forget that taking a small break or walking away from something is not only okay but might be the wisest choice.

Opening and closing is not an all-or-nothing practice. We don't have to be fully open or fully closed. We can switch and adjust the amount of opening and closing as we need to. For example, one day you may feel fully open to reading or doing an exercise, whereas another day you may notice a little resistance. Resistance can feel like frustration, anger, numbing, or an emotional wall. Sometimes we feel resistance strongly, sometimes we feel it a little bit. And that is perfectly okay. Allow yourself to be and feel as you are with this book. Very often our emotions and experiences, including resistance, might be trying to tell us something. Perhaps that something painful may be coming up for you, like a thought, a memory, a previous or ongoing trauma.[2] Give yourself a break if you need it. Your emotions are wise, as are you.

To help you along your journey, there will be seven other Super-Women alongside you, as a kind of a support group, learning and processing the various skills illustrated here. Although their names and interactions are fictional, their stories are real, shared with permission, to support you throughout your journey.

In addition, other Super-Women from all over the world also wanted to contribute their stories to help you on your journey. Throughout this book, you will find their quotes and stories in the chapter sidebars. These are all real quotes from real women around the world who sent in their stories specifically for you, to let you know that you are not alone, to let you know that they are with you on this journey.

You will be invited to participate and interact with the characters in this book. Feel free to participate as much as you feel comfortable. In this sanctuary, you are fully accepted, exactly as you are. In this sanctuary, you are safe. In this sanctuary, you are unconditionally loved.

Perhaps take a few moments to design your sanctuary. It is okay if you are feeling self-conscious about this exercise. This exercise, this space, this is just for you. No one else is here to judge you. No one else is here to tell you what to do. This is your space. And in this space you are free to be yourself.

Imagine what your safe space might look like and how it might feel. Some people like to imagine that their sanctuary is a cabin with a fireplace, or a quiet place near the beach, or perhaps a quiet nook full of books and warm tea or coffee, or a fictional place from your favorite fandom.

Some people have a difficult time envisioning their safe space. If that is true for you, that's okay too. Start slow; perhaps imagine a place you would like to visit and what elements you would like there.

What would your sanctuary look like?

Superhero Training Step: If and when you feel comfortable, write down your own description of what your sanctuary might look like. This place can be real, imagined, or fictional. You are welcome to imagine yourself being in a fantastical place you read about in a book or saw in a movie, or to design your own. Think about what kind of an environment it would be. Would it be outdoors in nature or indoors at a cozy cabin or a nook? What would be around you? What would the temperature be? Would it be warm and sunny or cold but cozy with lots of warm blankets and a rocking chair? This is your space; feel free to design it any way that would make you wish to be there, in any way that would make you feel safe there. A shelf of books, candles or some calming music? Would you want to be alone in your safe space or have anyone with you? Perhaps your pet or another loved one? Would you want to enjoy the sound of silence, nature, or soft music? Take a few moments to reflect on and design your sanctuary, perhaps write down what it might look like, and see if you can envision yourself arriving there.

Chapter 2

Your Origin Story

Welcome to the sanctuary. This is your space to explore yourself and work on your superhero training to empower the Super-Woman that you are. You will not be going through this experience alone. Just as a gentle reminder, there will be seven other women in the group with you. Are you ready to meet them?

Let's take a moment and meet the whole group.

Please take a moment and introduce yourselves.

Most people think that superheroes are fictional characters with supernatural abilities. And it is true that some of the superheroes we read about and see in movies and television shows have some kind of superpower. However, not all superheroes do. I imagine you can probably name a number of superheroes who do not have superpowers in the traditional sense, but use their intelligence, science, technology, compassion, observation, and other skills to help others.

When people learn that I practice Superhero Therapy, most assume two things: that I only focus on talking about traditional superheroes in therapy, and that I work with children. Neither of those is true. Superhero Therapy came out of work with active-duty service members who were experiencing post-traumatic stress disorder (PTSD). Now, I primarily work with adult clients, and as a Superhero therapist (a person providing Superhero Therapy) my goal is to help people to realize their superhero potential and become a superhero in real life (IRL).

Everyone has an origin story, and most superheroes have a traumatic origin story.[3] In fact, many heroes' journeys begin with a loss, a trauma, abuse, or a life-changing hurt. It is in facing this pain and growing—not just despite but *because* of it—that some superheroes are made.

Many origin stories are painful, most of them are life-changing. It is a part of the human experience. For some of us, an origin story may have been a significant loss in our childhood, or perhaps it was years of emotional, physical, or sexual abuse.

Some of these origin stories may be relatable, some may be difficult to read. At any point, if you need to soothe and support yourself, give yourself the permission to focus on your breathing, perhaps even closing your eyes, and take as much time as you need until you feel ready to continue. Give yourself the permission to read and participate as much or as little as you feel safe doing, and allow yourself to take a break at any time and take as long as you need before returning to the group. Imagine yourself alone in your sanctuary or with a support person or a pet.

Would anyone be willing to go first?

Zaara raises her hand, volunteering to share her origin story.

Zaara's origin story

"My family moved here from Pakistan. And although I was born here, I was severely bullied in school. Kids in my classes tormented me, yelling at me, 'Go back to your country!' even though I tried telling them that I was in the country in which I was born. I hid in my room, having no friends for years. I was so depressed during middle school that I often thought about suicide.

"Things got better as I got older. I started making friends in high school and then found myself in college. I found that my college classmates were a lot more accepting and supportive than kids in my middle school and even high school. I also found that they were less cliquey, so I was able to find and establish friendships.

"I was feeling much better, my depression was almost entirely gone. And then it happened. I was assaulted by one of my classmates. It was as if everything went black. The sky looked black to me. I felt like I was breathing ash. I was suffocating. I was terrified to tell anyone because sexual assault is not always well understood in some Muslim communities. Women are sometimes shamed, often by other women, for experiencing it. I was afraid of what would happen to me if my story got out. I was afraid of what would happen if my parents found out. I was scared that the shame of this situation might cause them grief within their community.

"So, I never reported it.

"Three years later, I still feel like I am in my own prison. Sometimes I am scared to go to campus, afraid that I will see him again. I have not had a gynecological exam since it happened. I tried once and left. I am scared every day. I try to avoid male students, male professors, male TAs, and anyone who might remind me of him. I feel stuck and I can't keep going like this."

There is a silence in the room as the rest of the group members are breathing, processing the depth of Zaara's story. Tala agrees to go next.

Tala's story

"Zaara, I am so glad you shared your story. I wasn't sure if I should bring up my own assault. Mine happened in high school with a person I dated. I didn't know that I had the right to be upset, because when I tried to tell my friend, she said, 'Well, you're dating, so it's not *rape* rape.'

"However, my origin story began in my childhood. My family and I moved here from the Philippines when I was three years old. Growing up, I was expected to take care of my brothers and sisters, and learned early on that my emotions weren't *allowed.* I was not allowed to feel angry, sad, scared, or any other emotions except happy. When I would try to tell my mother about my feeling depressed, she would shame me, stating that I have no right to feel that way after everything she had sacrificed for me. Somehow, I would end up apologizing and feeling worse than I already did.

"When my father left my mother for another woman, she told me that I always have to be on guard. She taught me not to trust men, because according to her, all men will want to cheat on me. She also taught me not to trust women because, according to her, all women would want to steal my partner and 'You're not pretty enough to keep his interest forever,' she would frequently add. I spent years comparing myself to other women, distrusting those whom I thought were prettier than me, and went through many relationships in which I could not trust my partner not to cheat on me. I am starting to see the toxic patterns of what I learned, and I want to break it."

Several women are tearing up now, and Hannah gently pats Tala's arm. Hannah agrees to share her story next.

Hannah's story

"Hearing your stories, I have to say that my heart goes out to both of you. I have thankfully never been sexually assaulted, but I used to work as a waitress and I used to deal with sexual harassment on a regular basis. Male customers would often talk to me about their sexual fantasies, and I would try to brush it off and focus on my job, but it made me feel unsafe and uncomfortable.

"As for an origin story, I guess it started gradually. I was always an anxious kid, but after my grandmother died suddenly—I must have been eight years old—I started to worry about my family dying. I cried myself to sleep, worrying that when I would wake up, someone in my family would die. I started doing everything I could to keep them safe. I would tell myself that so long as I counted all the broccoli on my plate, they would be safe. I thought that so long as I gave them four kisses, they would be safe. After a while, my OCD became this unmanageable monster. My parents took me to see a psychologist and I learned skills that helped me cope much better and my OCD symptoms significantly reduced. However, since my daughter was born, they have all returned with a vengeance. I constantly worry that I will do something to hurt my child or that something will happen to her. I check on her every hour at night, I take her to a pediatrician for every rash, bump, or sneeze. Over the past month, I started having thoughts that I might harm her somehow and I cannot get them out of my mind. It's gotten so bad that I am afraid to go near her, and my husband and nanny take care of her now. She cries for me and I don't know how to bring myself to hold her. My family shames me. They call me a bad mother. They say I am selfish. My husband threatens to leave me. I don't know how to make them understand that I am terrified of hurting my baby but that I never actually want to do that."

Hannah sobs, her head in her hands. Both Tala and Isabella rub her back gently. After a few minutes, Hannah stops crying and blows her nose.

"Thank you," she says. "I get so scared of sharing this with others."

I remind her gently, "People with OCD, especially people who experience what's called *harm OCD,* obsessively worry about hurting others precisely because they never ever want to do it. People who actually hurt other people usually don't fixate on it."

"Right. Okay." She sniffles and smiles through the tears.

Isabella agrees to share next.

Isabella's story

"Like many other people, I too experienced sexual assault. More than one. But that is not why I am here.

"I am here because I am trying to find out who I am. I feel torn between all parts of me. I am from Chiapas but was raised in the USA. I consider myself neither fully Mexican, nor fully American. In conversations with people from both cultures, I find myself feeling like an outsider. I am bisexual and am not feeling accepted in the straight nor in the gay community. I have been asked to choose and told that I have to. My most recent partner was a guy who told me that I am 'kidding myself' with my sexuality. I am a hairdresser with no hair, a woman without breasts, a cancer survivor but the chemo effects have persisted. I am neither sick nor healthy. I feel like I do not know who I am. And I am hoping to find pieces of myself and glue them together because I am tired of feeling shattered."

Isabella squeezes her hands together on her own lap and closes her eyes, breathing. We all take a few moments to breathe together, and soon our breath synchronizes, so that we all breathe in unison—connected to one another through our inhalation and exhalation, creating a safe space for one another.

After a few moments, Isabella's eyes open and she nods that she is ready to keep going. Victoria agrees to share her story.

Victoria's story

"I have seen a lot of violence in my life, most of it in my own home. Most of it directed at me. In addition to my dad beating on me and my brother, I got into more fights than I can count in school. The teacher would always let the white kids share their side of the story first, and I was marked as 'aggressive.' It didn't matter that they started it. It didn't matter that they called me the 'N-word.' I was automatically perceived to be at fault. Once in my history class, I brought up how racism is still prevalent today. My teacher told me that it's hardly prevalent at all and that I should be grateful to be living during such an accepting time.

"Growing up, before my transition, I was the one everyone feared. I had the police called on me more times than I can count. People would cross the street when they'd see me or reach for their phones when I was simply passing them.

"It bothered me, sure. But I never thought that after my transition I would go from being feared to fearing for my life. My first assault happened six months after starting my hormones. That was only the first. That was when I realized that I was unsafe and things I never thought of before, such as walking down the street by myself, became dangerous to me. I lost two friends last year, both of them trans, both to hate crimes. I am scared for my life and I am scared that when people look at me, they don't actually see me for what I am: a human being. Someone who just wants what anyone else wants: acceptance and safety. People still misgender me, referring to me as a man, despite me repeatedly correcting them. Sometimes I wonder if it's okay for me to expect others to see me as I am: a woman. Sometimes I don't think I do. On those days, I fear that one day I may take my own life."

Victoria breathes heavily for a short time, pressing her lips. She then closes her eyes for a few moments, focusing on her breathing just like we practiced. She slows down her breathing to soothe and support herself. After a few minutes, she opens her eyes. She swallows, her sadness evident in her posture. She takes a few more breaths and nods that she is ready for us to continue.

After a few moments, Lisa volunteers next.

Lisa's story

"Like many of you here, I have been assaulted too but that is not the main reason why I am here." She sighs, takes a breath, and then continues. "My entire life, my family's focus has been on my weight. Since I was four years old, I was chastised for eating too much and told that I needed to practice portion control. I was eight when my mom sent me to fat camp, despite me pleading with her not to. To this day, our conversations begin and end with a discussion about my weight.

"My mom has bought me memberships to multiple gyms and signed me up for so many weight-loss programs. I used to barely eat. I almost died from an eating disorder. I hate the idea of food and yet, because of my family, I am always worried about what I might eat and how that might translate to my weight. I am a lawyer. I have two doctorates, but that is not enough. My parents, my friends, many of my doctors, and most of my exes could only see me for my weight.

"Last year, I went to see my doctor about the pain in my side. He said that I have to lose weight. It turned out that I had appendicitis. When I saw my doctor for my headaches, I was prescribed diet and exercise, when the pain was actually caused by the intense stress I was under in law school. I look at people who are thinner than me as 'better than me,' almost like they are in a different class. I hate going shopping and I hate seeing doctors. I don't want my identity to be tied to the number on my scales. I feel depressed and worthless most of the time, and I am sick and tired of feeling that way."

Lisa's lips are pursed. Her breathing is faster now than when she started speaking. She closes her eyes and takes a few minutes to breathe, allowing her anger and frustration to settle. When she opens her eyes again, her breathing has slowed down, and she nods to continue. Divya goes next.

Divya's story

"For the longest time, I thought that my job was to be a wife and a mother. I went through two miscarriages and did not think that I would be able to get pregnant. Both miscarriages felt like a death. No one else could understand and people would tell me it's common to have a miscarriage, but I grieved. Then I was able to give birth, and I have two daughters now. I love being a wife and a mother, but now I also want more. I have been studying to be an architect. I'm doing my master's degree now. Most of my classes are online but some advanced classes are on campus.

"My husband is unhappy with me taking classes outside of the house. We have been fighting and it has been putting a strain on our marriage. My migraines have also been becoming more frequent. I have multiple sclerosis, fibromyalgia, and have had migraines since I was a small child, but recently my pain has gotten so strong that I can barely function. The pain has made it impossible to take care of my husband, my children, my parents, and to do my classes as well. I am stressed, I am constantly in pain, I don't know what to do. Most people look at me and assume that I am healthy because they cannot see my pain, but the truth is, I am never okay. I am always hurting."

Divya looks down for a few moments and then looks up again, ready to continue.

Superhero Training Step: If and when you feel comfortable, feel free to write down your own origin story. Please give yourself the permission to write as much or as little as you would like. This is your story, as told from your point of view, your experiences, and your reactions to them. You are the expert in it. I believe you and I believe in you. The advantage of writing your origin story is that it allows you the chance to externalize it, meaning that you can take it outside of yourself and look at it, perhaps noticing how much it has affected you and which aspects of it still affect you the most. At any point, if you need to take a breath or a break, give yourself the permission to do so. Take as much time as you need with this practice.

Thank you for sharing your story. As you can see, all eight of you experienced extremely painful events and all eight of you are the epitome of what it takes to be a superhero. At numerous times in your life, you have displayed tremendous courage and overcome what seemed impossible.

Now that we have identified your origin story, we are going to take a look at how it might have affected you and learn ways in which we can find strength in our experiences.

Chapter 3

Building Emotional Safety

Anyone can be affected by certain events. Fictional characters are often built and developed by their past experiences, and many of us function the same way. Sometimes, we may not even notice a reaction we are having to a particular situation unless we are feeling triggered or overwhelmed. Emotional safety is a way to notice and experience our emotions in a safe way. In order to allow ourselves to find and experience emotional safety, it can be helpful to track how we react to certain situations, so that we can start noticing changes when they are first occurring and learn techniques for soothing and supporting ourselves.

All events we experience may affect how we feel, how we think, and what we do. Understanding this relationship between our thoughts, feelings, and behaviors can help to reduce trauma reactions and break the trigger pattern over time.[4]

Thoughts, feelings, and behaviors can all affect one another bidirectionally. Thoughts are the way that we interpret an event, such as thinking that someone may be angry with us if they ignore our text or call. Feelings are emotions that we experience, such as feeling sad, angry, happy, scared, or insecure. In addition, feelings can also include physiological sensations, such as a pounding heart or feeling out of breath or light-headed. Finally, behaviors are the actions that we take or avoid taking; for example, canceling plans to go out when we are feeling anxious is a behavior.

As mentioned above, thoughts, feelings, and behaviors all affect one another. For example, someone who was emotionally abused by their mother may have triggering reactions to being criticized by, or even receiving feedback from, older women. In this case, the critical feedback can lead to thoughts such as "I messed up again. I am never good enough. I am a failure" and therefore feeling ashamed, embarrassed, angry, and frustrated. As a result, an individual going through these experiences may withdraw, shut down, become defensive, snap, or leave the room. These are behaviors.

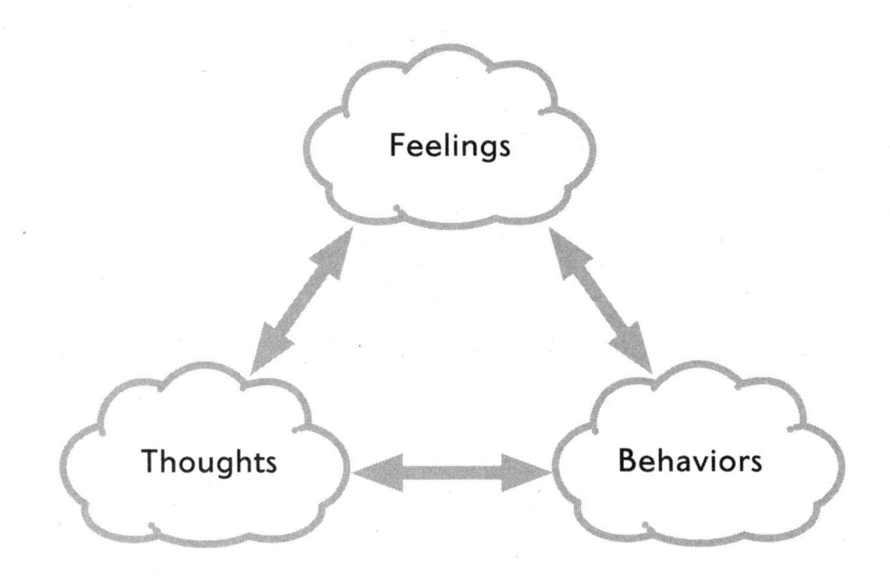

Can any of you relate to that?

"I can definitely relate to that," Tala says. "If I ever forgot to put away my clothes, my mother would tell me that I was a terrible daughter, that I was a pig and a slob. Now, whenever someone tells me to clean up after myself, I get furious with them and snap at them."

"It's completely understandable that after experiencing criticism for many years, you may automatically react to someone's comment in this way," I say. "What thoughts come up for you when someone is being critical?"

Tala considers this for a moment. "I'm not sure. I just feel like they are judging me."

"Okay, so the thought you have is that they are judging you?"

"I guess. Yes," Tala responds.

"And of course, when we think that someone is judging us, we may feel angry and defensive, and may react by snapping or by not wanting to be around someone whom we perceive as trying to hurt us in some way. Let's take a moment and identify the elements that come up for you in this example."

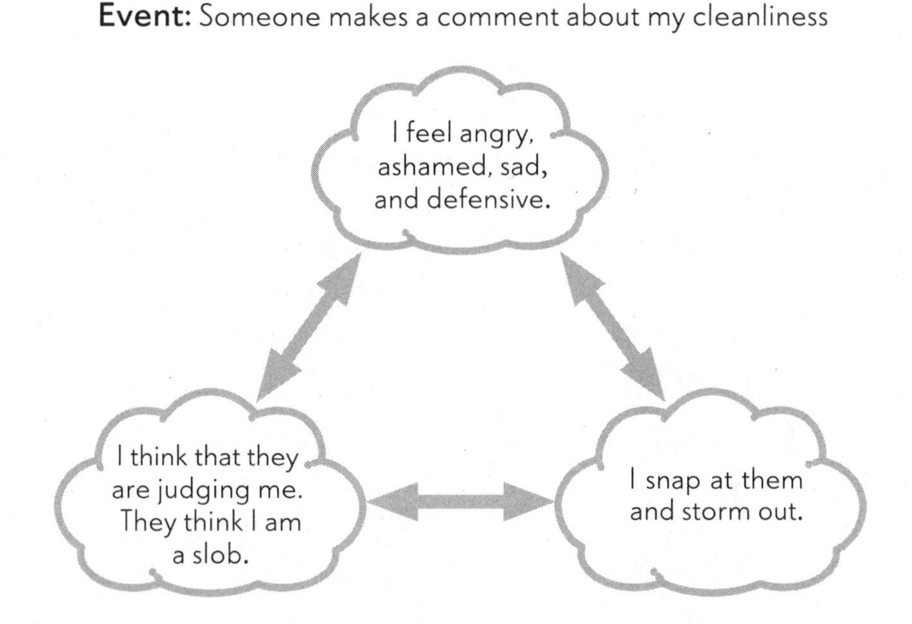

Usually we go through our day without considering these components until they become impossible to ignore. When we experience strong emotions, such as anger, shame, depression, emotional numbing, overwhelming anxiety, or frustration, it usually means that we need something. By paying attention to ourselves and investigating what we might need, we can build our emotional safety and support ourselves during a difficult time.

Some of the factors that can influence how we feel and what we need include biological, psychological, social, situational, and behavioral factors, as well as the amount and the availability of necessary resources to be able to cope with them.

Biological factors include chronic illness (such as chronic pain disorder, chronic fatigue syndrome, multiple sclerosis, and other disorders), physical disability, as well as biological predisposition for certain psychological disorders, such as depression. Biological factors also can include the genetic predisposition to the way our bodies react to stress, the way we process food, our height, weight, and certain aspects of our appearance. Sadly, we might sometimes be harassed, bullied, or shame ourselves for having the biological factors that we have no control over.

Our biological factors include our basic survival needs, such as our need to eat, sleep, hydrate, move, and rest. When these are not met, we are likely to experience burnout, depression, stress, physical pain, irritability, and/or panic attacks. As uncomfortable as these reactions may be, they are often helpful in alerting us that we may need something. By paying attention to these reactions, we may be able to notice what we are feeling and what we need. For example, when we continuously work, take care of others, feel the time pressure, and don't have time to eat or rest, we may experience *burnout*. Burnout refers to physical and/or emotional exhaustion, which can lead to both psychological and physiological distress.[5]

Burnout can lead to:

- Reduced caring about yourself or others
- Irritability, anger, or frustration
- Feeling lethargic
- Being impatient and less empathic toward others
- Reduced satisfaction with your job, work, or family
- Wanting to quit your job or leave a relationship
- And, sometimes, thoughts of suicide

"I can relate to that," Divya says. "When I've spent all day cleaning, doing laundry, doing the dishes, cooking, and studying, my pain gets so bad that I can barely move. I am still trying to do my homework and I am stressed about getting my work done on time. And when my husband comes home from work and wants me to bring him dinner from the kitchen instead of getting it himself, my pain gets much worse, as does my frustration with him."

"Thank you for sharing that, Divya," I tell her. "We often put so much pressure on ourselves to do everything on our to-do list, that we may often neglect our own needs. What might be a biological need that you may have when your pain gets worse?"

She thinks about it for a moment. "I think... to rest? But if I don't bring him dinner, my husband would get angry with me and start telling me that he works all day and I just lie around and do nothing."

"And how do you feel when he says that?"

"Angry! So angry. He doesn't see how hard I am working and how much pain I am in. And if I try to tell him about it, he just tells me that I need to quit school. But I don't want to do that. So, I just don't say anything anymore and just give him his dinner and keep doing my homework."

When others do not understand what we need and when it may be difficult to meet our own needs, we may feel angry, and at times our pain, physical or emotional, may become significantly worse. Such pain increase is a way of alerting us that our resources are depleting and that we may need to rest and nurture ourselves. We will talk more about how to do that later. In the meantime, let's talk about other factors.

Another factor that can affect us is our **thoughts**. Most people spend most of their time thinking about the awful things that occurred in the past and worrying about the potentially terrifying things that might occur in the future. We often worry about getting hurt, rejected, misunderstood, or criticized, even though in the current moment that threat may not be present.

Some of our thoughts are helpful, such as thoughts about setting and following important goals. In fact, the inverse of what we usually worry about points to what we truly care about. For example, when a friend does not return our text, we may have a thought that they are angry with us. This fear points to how important this friendship may be and how much we value it. However, other thoughts may be less helpful, such as thoughts about the worst possible scenario (catastrophizing thoughts) and thoughts about whether or not other people may be judging us (mind-reading thoughts). Other thoughts can be harsh and self-invalidating, such as *I am a failure, I am not good enough, I should never make mistakes,* and *If people actually get to know the real me, they will reject me.*

There are many reasons why these thoughts develop. Sometimes, these thoughts come from what we have been taught by our family or within our environment. These thoughts might also develop from our fears of being rejected and abandoned. To be accepted, to feel unconditionally loved, to feel like we belong is a basic human need, and it makes sense that we might fear losing our fundamental support groups. Thus, we might be highly vigilant to ensure that it does not happen. Such fears and anxieties about feeling rejected and losing your immediate support person(s) are more likely to happen if you have experienced emotional abuse, neglect, or invalidation from people who were in charge of taking care of you as a child.

In fact, most of our painful thoughts are an attempt to preserve our emotional safety. Feeling unheard, misunderstood, heartbroken, or rejected can feel like a death because as humans, we are meant for love and connection. In the past, humans existed in kinship-based social groups, and getting rejected from one's group back then would lead to almost certain death. Nowadays, we may be less dependent on others for survival than we used to be. However, most of us are still wired to thrive in supportive social environments. In addition, some of us may also be in a situation in which leaving our current social group may not be safe or possible. So, it is understandable that if we are unable to receive the love and connection from the people in our social group, we may feel devastated and alone. And of course, it makes perfect sense that if we have ever experienced the excruciating pain of rejection, then we may be terrified of feeling it again and therefore spend most of our time worrying about and trying to find ways to prevent it from happening.

Have any of you experienced that?

"I have," Hannah says. "I worry all the time. I worry about what could happen if I make a mistake with my child. I constantly worry about getting angry or frustrated around my child. I guess I catastrophize about hurting her and I'm scared to be around her."

"Thank you for bringing up that example, Hannah," I tell her. "We said earlier that the inverse of our fears is often our core value. What core values might be represented here in your fears?"

Hannah thinks about it for a moment. "Hmm. I guess that I value being a good mom to Sarah. I value being able to care for others and I fear that I might make a mistake."

"Very wise of you to notice that," I respond to her. "When we care about something or someone, we may sometimes worry about doing something wrong, often neglecting any evidence that shows us how well we are performing already."

Hannah looks up at me. "I guess that's true. I almost never focus on all the great times with Sarah that I've had in the past."

Our thoughts might sometimes be affected by our **social environment**. Sometimes we might be in a toxic and invalidating environment in which people may judge us, put us down, or hurt us, making us feel unsafe and unwanted. For example, people might say, *You bring shame to our family, You're too sensitive, What is wrong with you?* or *You're crazy.* Unfortunately, many people, especially women, are likely to hear all or some of these phrases in their lives at a time when they are most in need of love and support.

At other times, well-meaning but misguided individuals in our lives may offer unhelpful advice, such as *Just don't think about it,* or *You shouldn't feel that way, Other people have it much worse than you, You should be happy*, and *At least it's not as bad as it could have been.* While all of these may be intended to be helpful, none of them really are because ultimately all of them translate to *Your experience is wrong, You are not allowed to have your experience,* and *You are not accepted for having your experience.*

"Oh, my gosh! That's how I used to feel with my family when they were still talking to me," Isabella says. "They would always tell me that at least my cancer is not terminal. They would tell me that I am too sensitive. They would say that I've brought shame on our family because of my sexual orientation. But they didn't even see me. It felt like being me is not allowed. Like *I'm* not allowed." She breathes as she cries, squeezing her fists.

A few moments later, Zaara speaks. Her voice is trembling. "My parents never said it to me directly, but I know that if they ever found out about my sexual assault, they would be ashamed of me. They tell me about other women and young girls who were assaulted. Only they don't talk about the girls' pain. They talk about how much shame those girls bring upon their families and how they worry about the girls' parents and their reputations. I don't know how to tell them that whatever may happen to the parents, it is so much worse for the person who was assaulted."

She looks shaken. I feel my own heart breaking for both of them. "Thank you both for your courage in sharing your stories. It's heartbreaking when in the times of our greatest suffering, we may not always be able to receive support from the people closest to us." They both nod. "What do you both need right now?"

"To breathe," Isabella says.

"To feel safe," Zaara responds.

We all breathe for a few moments... Not rushing... Allowing any and all emotions to be present. Allowing all of you to be as open or as closed as you feel safe being.

I wait for all of you to look up, nodding that you are ready before we continue.

Clearly, emotional support is very important in making us feel safe and comfortable. At times when social support is present, it can become a powerful factor in helping our mental health. At times when it is absent, it can be more challenging to meet our struggles on our own. At those times we may benefit from creating our own communities. For example, some people join in-person support groups. Others find an online network, where they might be able to receive the support they are looking for. Still others may find support through fictional characters, which can function as our own surrogate family or friends. In fact, some people say that they might feel more connected and understood by fictional characters than by people in their own lives.

"Yep," Victoria says. "Growing up, I didn't know any other trans people. But there was this trans superhero, Real-Girl. She was all about being authentic even if others didn't agree with her. Reading about her journey to find herself gave me the courage to do it too. It was almost like she was talking directly to me in the comics. The things she said were the things I always wanted to hear from other people."

"Thank you so much for sharing that, Victoria," I say. "It is so powerful that at a time when it was difficult for you to find someone to connect with, you were able to find and establish a beautiful connection with this superhero. Many people might feel the same way. Where our own support systems may sometimes fail us, our fictional connections may sometimes say the exact phrase we so long to hear. What was that phrase for you?"

Victoria smiles. "*Be who you are because you are enough.* I cried when I read that page. I have it framed in my room."

People, and even fictional characters, can sometimes affect how we feel. In addition, certain situations can also influence how we might feel and how we might act. For example, when we are running late, we might be less patient with ourselves and others than we might be when we are not in a rush. Other factors that might affect us include the food that we eat, the beverages we drink, and even the weather that changes around us. Some people are more sensitive to these than others. For example, some people might feel more anxious or more depressed when the weather changes. Some people might have *seasonal affective disorder*—a condition in which you can experience significant mood changes during certain seasons, such as the cold winter months or the hot summer months. In addition, some people might experience an increase in physical pain, mental fog, and emotional distress when the weather changes.

"That's right," Divya says. "My migraines and mental fog both get a lot worse before it rains."

"I don't usually talk about it, but I get very depressed when the weather changes," Lisa says.

"That's not uncommon," I say to them both. "Many people are affected by weather changes. Some people might feel depressed, while others might feel anxious, angry, or irritable during certain times of the year or when the weather changes. Some people feel worse when it's raining, while others feel worse when it is sunny out. By noticing how we respond to certain events, we might be more able to give ourselves what we need to get through it."

Another factor that can affect how we feel and think, as well as what happens to us, has to do with the choices we make. We refer to this factor as the **behavioral factor**. In most situations we may have some choices as to how we respond to the situation that is occurring. In others, our choices may be limited. Sometimes, our choices may all lead to outcomes we may not like or want. Being able to notice the choices we are making, as well as all the possible choices that we have, can allow us to take the kind of action that would be most helpful in order for us to meet our needs.

The behavioral factor does not only have to do with the actions we choose to take—it also includes the actions we choose *not* to take. For example, when we experience panic attacks, we may avoid going very far from our safety zone, which might be our house. Although some avoidance behaviors may be helpful in terms of avoiding toxic situations (for example, avoiding being around someone who is abusive), avoidance of our thoughts and emotions can sometimes backfire. For example, avoidance of grief can actually intensify our grief reactions over time, potentially leading to depression, anger outbursts, or panic attacks.

In order to figure out how our behaviors might affect us, let's take a look at some coping behaviors that we might sometimes engage in in response to stressful situations. All of them are ways in which we may sometimes seek safety. None of these behaviors are "good" or "bad." We are just looking to see which behaviors are common for us and what our needs might be when these responses happen.

Coping behaviors:

- Shutting down/withdrawing during an argument or after receiving negative feedback
- Leaving the room/environment
- Calling a friend
- Avoiding going somewhere for the fear that you may feel too uncomfortable being there
- Threatening to leave
- Asking for reassurance
- Cutting, hair pulling, or skin picking
- Taking a bath
- Snuggling with your pets
- Asking for a hug
- Setting a boundary
- Yelling
- Reading a book
- Using substances (food, alcohol, drugs, cigarettes) for emotion management
- Watching TV
- Playing video games
- Doing a meditation

- Going to yoga or working out
- Canceling a meeting
- Taking medication
- Going on social media
- Writing fan fiction

All of these behaviors can happen as a direct response to needing emotional safety. These coping behaviors can sometimes serve as an immediate short-term relief for an excruciatingly painful experience. For some of us, some of these tools, including substance use, could be all the tools that we have, all that we know. And perhaps for some of us, they have been the only tools that have allowed us to temporarily meet our needs, keep us safe, keep us from suicide. As you can see, some of these tools might have even functioned as a survival mechanism. Some of them can continue to be helpful over time and some might become problematic over time. We are going to be learning more tools to add to your superhero utility belt for use when you are struggling.

Both emotional safety, as well as a connection with our loved ones and our passions, are critical in allowing us to embark on our heroic quest. Thus, the formula to being a superhero is:

Superheroing = connection + safety

This means that connection to who we are, as well as connection to our loved ones, our passions, and our core values is the core of human existence and is the core of being a superhero. However, when we are facing an overwhelming amount of physical or emotional pain, it is just as important to find support for ourselves in order to aid us through our superhero journey. Therefore, superheroing is essentially finding a balance between our sense of connection to the most vital parts of our life and our emotional safety.

In working on establishing our sense of emotional safety, we may need to consider what we are going through. Identifying and noticing our thoughts, feelings, and behaviors can allow us to be more mindful of our needs and can reduce the intensity of our experience over time. Allowing ourselves to name and notice these experiences can allow us to find a way to work on self-soothing and creating emotional safety for ourselves. Let's try a brief exercise of mindfully identifying the various factors that might affect us in some way.

There is absolutely no pressure to complete this exercise if you don't want to. If you would like to try it out, read about each factor and then write about your own experience with it. You can use a journal (paper or digital), or download and print out a PDF version of the exercise at http://www.newharbinger.com/47520. Feel free to write as much or as little as you feel comfortable doing. This is your safe space. In this space, whatever you feel is right, and all your experiences are allowed.

Factor	Explanation	Examples
Biological	Chronic physical condition; disability, illness, genetic predisposition; also sleep, thirst, hunger, and burnout	Isabella's cancer condition; Divya's chronic pain and burnout
Cognitive (our thoughts)	Our interpretations of the situation	Tala thinking that she is not good enough to be loved
Emotional	Typically one-word names given to our specific feelings, such as sad, angry, or frustrated	Zaara feeling anxious about telling her family about the assault. Anxiety is an emotion here, whereas the belief that her parents will not understand her is a thought
Social	The way that our interactions with others affect us	Lisa's family shaming her over her weight; Victoria experiencing prejudice and misgendering

Situational	Circumstances that may be out of our control, such as the weather, unemployment, or not having enough time, resources, or support	Divya's pain being affected by the weather
Behavioral	What we do, resist doing, or avoid doing	Hannah avoiding holding her child

Mindfulness as a way of creating physical and emotional safety

Because we are wired to keep ourselves safe, it makes sense that our mind will try to do everything possible to protect us. Our mind is constantly assessing the risks around us in preparation for action. In some situations, such risk assessment may be helpful, especially if we are continuously in an unsafe or invalidating environment. In that case, having an idea of possible outcomes can help us to prepare and to keep ourselves as safe as possible. However, in other situations this constant future monitoring may not be helpful, as we may spend 99 percent of our mental time and attention trying to prevent something that hardly ever happens. This is where mindfulness comes in.

Mindfulness is a way of noticing our thoughts, feelings, sensations, and the environment around us. Mindfulness means paying attention to ourselves and our surroundings in a gentle and nonjudgmental way. This practice is the first step to creating emotional safety because it allows us to know *when* we are struggling, so that we can determine *what* we might need. For example, noticing your body tension, especially in your jaw and shoulders, could indicate that you may feel stressed or anxious. Allowing yourself to breathe, soothing your muscle tension, can help you feel more grounded in the present moment.

Not all emotions and sensations that we feel are the enemy, even though we might not like some of them. Our experiences are informative—they are indicators of what we might need in that particular moment.

"I don't understand how my OCD is helpful or informative," Hannah says.

"What are some of the main emotions that come up for you when your OCD symptoms increase?" I ask her.

"Anxiety and absolute panic."

"And when you feel those emotions, Hannah, what do you need at that time? What do you yearn for?"

"Hmm. I've never really thought about it in terms of need. I guess... to feel safe, to know that everything is going to be okay, that my family is safe."

> I "flatlined" in my father's arms after a lengthy seizure at seventeen months old, but medical professionals were able to resuscitate me at the emergency room. I now can hear, smell, and feel things that most people cannot. I have a very hard time tuning out stimuli to this day. It used to be very hard for me to regulate emotion in the face of that overload. For some time, I had difficulty determining what was safe and not safe in terms of what to do and where to go, because my body was reacting to everything all the time.
>
> What's been helpful for me is meditation, reflection, healthy diet and exercise, writing, talking to other people about it—including a therapist and my parents. I would say let people in your bubble, push out the sides of your bubble, but also always know when to pull back in and know that it is a strong shield. Know that you are all you need to defend yourself, to stand up for yourself, and to fight for the rights of others.
>
> —"Bubble Girl"

We are constantly receiving information from our body about what we need. Most of us go through our day not noticing (or even actively avoiding) our emotions and sensations. Mindfulness is the opposite of that. Mindfulness gently invites us to observe our physical, emotional, cognitive, and sensory experiences to see what we are feeling, thinking, and perceiving. All our input is informative and our emotions usually function to allow us to learn about our needs.

Here are some emotions that most people experience at least some of the time. These emotions are neither "good" nor "bad." They just are. They usually signal a function or a need that we have in that moment.

Take a look at the table below and see if you can identify some of your own experiences with these emotions and what your needs might have been in those times. Write about your experiences in a journal (paper or digital), or download and print out a PDF version of this exercise at http://www.newharbinger.com/47520.

Emotion	Function	Need
Angry	To protect us against a threat, seeking safety or peace	Safety from the threat or to find peace
Anxious	To find safety and/or reassurance	Safety, soothing, comfort, support
Ashamed	To try to fit in; to avoid being judged or rejected	Compassion, acceptance, soothing
Depressed	To try to heal from the painful emotional experience	Emotional safety, compassion, support
Disgusted	To avoid toxicity, including toxic food or relationships	Safety or distance from the toxic environment
Embarrassed	To try to fit in; to avoid being judged or rejected	Compassion, acceptance, soothing
Empathic	To connect with and help others	Connection
Excited	To feel joy in meaningful experiences	Savoring, celebration

Emotion	Function	Need
Frustrated	To expel energy when things are not going the way we'd like	Safety, break, rest, assistance, support
Guilty	To change unhelpful behavior in the future	Acceptance, compassion, soothing
Happy	To experience joy, to promote engagement in activities and connections we care about	Savoring, gratitude
Hateful	Comes from pain, functions to protect ourselves from further pain	Safety, distance from the hateful object, soothing, support
Hopeful	To motivate change	Encouragement, gratitude
Insecure	To make sure we are fitting in, to reduce the chance of being rejected	Emotional safety, compassion, support
Irritable	To signal us that we might need a break/support	Safety, break, rest, assistance, support
Jealous	To evaluate the safety of our connection; comes from pain and fear	Emotional safety, soothing, compassion
Overwhelmed	To signal us that we might need a break/support	Safety, break, rest, assistance, support
Panicked	To get us to safety; to enable action (studying for exams, for example)	Emotional safety, break, rest, support
Sad	To receive support	Compassion, acceptance, soothing

Emotion	Function	Need
Scared	To seek safety away from the threat	Safety, break, rest, support
Triggered	To evaluate risk and seek safety	Safety, soothing, comfort, support
Vulnerable	To connect with people or experiences that are most meaningful to us	Connection

"It seems that most of our emotions suggest that we need to find safety," Zaara says. "It's funny. I never thought about emotional safety before but that's what I really need. That's what I always need."

"Me too," Victoria agrees.

"Me too," Tala says. "I always worry that people will judge me and not want to be in my life anymore, or that my boyfriend will leave me or cheat on me. I always shamed myself for feeling jealous. I never realized that it stemmed from my need to feel safe in our relationship."

Most of us have the yearning need to be accepted, and when we aren't, or when we perceive we aren't, we might feel sad, angry, anxious, or ashamed, for example. Mindfully noticing these emotions can allow us to figure out what we might need.

Most people believe that to practice mindfulness, you have to empty your mind. That is not the case. In fact, we cannot actually empty our mind. Our mind was not designed that way. It is constantly working, assessing, planning, moving from one thought to another, evaluating one threat or another. We are especially designed to automatically think of things that have gone wrong in the past and can go wrong in the future. This is the default mode of our brain, which functions to keep us safe, to process what we are doing, as well as to ensure that we are able to meet our real or perceived expectations.[6]

This default mode is especially active when we do not have something to focus on.[7] For example, when we are completing an easy task, one that we have done on many occasions, such as walking, driving, or doing the dishes, we are more likely to engage in such past- or future-related thoughts compared to when we are completing a task that requires more of our attention. This means that we may frequently get distracted during a mindfulness exercise, including meditation practice. Thoughts and past experiences may pop up that might take us away from the practice. Noticing these thoughts, emotions, memories, and sensations is actually an important part of the meditation practice. When you notice that you got distracted by a thought, a memory, or a feeling, see if you can take a breath and gently return and refocus on your mindfulness practice. It may be helpful to keep refocusing on a particular sensation, such as the feeling of your feet or hands, whenever you get distracted, as a way to anchor your attention and allow you to return to your practice.

Let's take a few moments and practice mindfulness now. During this practice you will be invited to notice different sensations and emotions in your body. If at any point you feel triggered or too overwhelmed to continue, give yourself the permission to take a break from this practice, and feel free to return to it whenever you are ready.

The key here is that mindfulness is a *practice.* It is not meant to be perfect; we are not trying to accomplish, compete, or achieve anything specific. We are just gently focusing on our body and our sensations, being open and curious to see what may come up, and we can support ourselves in that moment.

To begin, take a few moments to sit comfortably. If possible, see if you can find a position that can allow you to have some stillness in the body without pushing yourself to sit too rigidly. If at any point you feel pain or discomfort in your body and need to adjust your posture, please give yourself the permission to do so.

Bring your attention to your breathing. Notice how your body is moving with each inhale and each exhale.

Take a moment to notice that at this moment, you are right here, in this space. In this moment, you are not late for anything, you are not in a rush to get anywhere, you are right here in this moment. In this moment, there is nothing else you need to do. In this moment, you are safe.

And at any time, if you get distracted or overwhelmed, you can silently ask yourself, "Where are my feet?" to gently bring yourself back to the present moment. Your feet (or your arms or lips if the sensation in your feet is inaccessible to you) will serve as an anchor point, allowing you to be more grounded, more rooted in this moment, reminding yourself that right now you are here, in this sanctuary. And right now, in this moment, you are safe.

Still focusing on your breathing, see if you can scan your body for any areas of pain or tension, beginning with your feet. If the sensation of your feet or any other parts of your body is inaccessible or uncomfortable to you, give yourself the permission to skip that part of the exercise.

Take a moment to notice if there is any pain or tension in your feet.

And then see if you can take a few slow breaths to focus on soothing your feet in this moment.

Then take a few moments to observe the sensations in your legs, starting with your ankles, calves, knees, and then thighs.

Take a few breaths here, notice any sensations you may be able to observe in this moment. And if you find yourself feeling distracted by a thought or a memory, gently and silently ask yourself, "Where are my feet?" allowing you to return to the present moment and to this exercise.

Take a few moments to breathe, noticing the sensations of your legs, allowing your legs to relax and soften.

Then, take a few moments to focus on the sensation of your hips and your lower back, just noticing how they feel right now. Notice any pain or tension in those areas. Take a few moments to breathe, noticing the sensations in these areas, allowing them to soothe and relax.

Then, take a few moments to focus on the sensation of your middle and upper back, just noticing how your back feels right now. Notice any pain or tension in your back. Take a few moments to breathe, noticing the sensations in these areas, allowing your back to soothe and relax.

Then, take a few moments to focus on the sensation of your stomach. Our stomach is where we process a lot of our emotions, including fear, shame, and anxiety. It is also where our intuition lives. So take some extra time to focus on your stomach. Notice if it feels tense, achy, hungry, churning, or nauseated, or if it feels settled. Perhaps even place your hands on your stomach if that feels comfortable to you.

Take extra time here to focus on your breathing and the sensations in your stomach. Allow your stomach to soothe and settle.

And then, when you are ready, try shifting your attention to your chest. Our chest is another area where we might process our emotions, including happiness, sadness, and the feeling of being overwhelmed. See if you can take a few moments here to notice any tightness or tension in your chest. Perhaps place one or both of your hands on your heart center if that feels comfortable to you. Just taking a few gentle moments here to notice the sensations of your chest as you are breathing in and breathing out, allow your chest to soften, letting go of some of its tension.

Then bring your attention to your arms, hands, and fingers. Just noticing how these areas feel right now. Noticing any pain or tension in these areas. Noticing if your fingers feel warm or cold. Perhaps spread out your fingers for a few moments, if that feels comfortable to you, and taking a few breaths, allow your hands to warm up with each breath. Take a few moments to allow these areas to relax and soften.

And then, relaxing your hands once more, place them down next to you or wherever you feel comfortable. And then bring your attention to your shoulders, your neck, and jaw. These areas often hold a lot of stress and tension. Take a few moments here to notice how these areas feel right now. Take some extra time to breathe, allowing these areas to soothe and soften.

Then, bring your attention to the sensations in your forehead, your temples, around your head, and on top of your head. Just notice how your head feels right now. Take a few moments to breathe, soothing and softening the muscles of your head, letting go of any tension you might observe there.

Continue to breathe as you shift your focus to your senses. If possible, take a few moments to notice any sounds around you while allowing yourself to gently breathe as you're doing so.

Now, if possible, take a few moments to notice if there are any smells you can detect in this environment, while continuing to breathe.

Now, take a few moments to notice the temperature in your environment, as you continue to gently breathe.

Perhaps take a few moments to gently look around, noticing your environment. Take your time with this practice, really observing the things around you, as if you've never been here before. Take a few moments to savor some beautiful things in your environment if possible. Notice any shapes, colors, or items you might be able to see, perhaps studying them for a few moments as if you've never seen them before.

Then, take a few moments to tune into your emotions. See if you can spend a few minutes trying to notice any emotions you may feel at this point. If you are not able to notice any emotions at this time, that's okay. If you do notice one or more emotions, see if you can gently and silently label them to yourself. For example: "That's anxiety. This is what anxiety feels like." Or "This is sadness. This is what sadness feels like."

See if you can take a few moments here, noticing any emotions that may be coming up for you. Our emotions are constantly changing. You might notice your emotions getting stronger or softer. See if you can notice them, observe them, allow them. And if at any point this practice exercise becomes too overwhelming, give yourself the permission to take a break, to refocus on the sensation of your breath, on the sensation of your feet, or another grounding sensation in your body. Allow yourself to find safety and stability in this moment.

Then, after a few moments, see if you can take some time to notice your thoughts. Sometimes we think in words, sometimes in pictures, movies, or concepts. See if you can notice the format of your thoughts. Allow yourself to breathe as you are gently focusing on your thoughts.

See if you can take a few moments to observe these thoughts, as if reading a book. Allow each thought to be like a sentence in a book—something you read and then notice, before then reading the next line.

Feel free to take a few minutes here, breathing and noticing your thoughts. And if you notice yourself getting overwhelmed or carried away by a thought, you can once more refocus on your breath or the sensation of your feet, finding stability and safety in this moment, if possible.

And then, when you are ready, take a few moments to let go of this practice, bringing your attention back to the sensation of your breath. Just notice the way that your body feels when you are breathing in and breathing out. Perhaps silently ask yourself, "What do I need right now? Do I need a break, a breath, some food, support, or nurturing?" And if the answer comes to you, see if you can reflect on it for a few moments. If no answer comes at this time, that is okay too.

And then bringing your awareness back to this room, notice yourself sitting, standing, or lying down, exactly as you are in this moment. Notice that right now, in this moment, you are right here. In this moment, you are safe.[1]

See if you can take a few breaths here, and whenever you are ready, feel free to gently let go of this practice, allowing yourself the permission to return to it at any time in the future.

What was this practice like for you?

1 If you are not safe in this moment, get yourself to safety immediately. Feel free to continue this exercise at a later time when you are in a safe environment.

Zaara is the first to speak. "I noticed that there were several times that I felt triggered when I was noticing my body. I am used to ignoring my body, so focusing on these sensations was hard. Feeling my body doesn't usually feel safe for me. When I was feeling triggered, I allowed myself to breathe through it and took a few breaks from the exercise."

"I started crying when you asked what we need. I am so used to asking others about what they need but I've never considered asking *myself*," Tala says.

Hannah nods. "I noticed that I was a lot more tense than I realized. I also noticed that my chest and my shoulders were very tense. They feel a little less tense now."

"I noticed that I am carrying a lot of sadness and I felt most of it in my chest," Isabella says.

Victoria shakes her head. "I had a really hard time. I kept getting distracted and overwhelmed. I felt a little calmer in the end, but this was a very difficult exercise for me. Like Zaara, feeling my body doesn't usually feel safe for me either."

"I noticed that I carry a lot of shame emotions in my stomach, so focusing on my body, especially my stomach, was very hard for me to do," Lisa says. "But it was interesting too. I never realized before that the very area I shame myself about is where my shame emotion lives."

"I noticed a lot of pain in my body, but also a lot of sadness," Divya says. "I didn't realize how sad I was feeling before. And similar to Tala, I've never before asked myself about what I need. This exercise was very difficult, but it was also nice."

Please take a moment to consider your experience during this practice, and, if you like, write something about it in your journal.

Sometimes, mindfulness practice can feel relaxing, at other times it might not. Mindfulness allows us to notice *ourselves* in the present moment, along with our experiences and needs. Most people report that, over time, practicing mindfulness becomes easier, more natural, like riding a bicycle or ice skating. However, even people with a lot of mindfulness experience will have a difficult time sometimes. The advantage of practicing mindfulness is that it allows us to notice what we may need in the moment and support ourselves, as well as to savor and appreciate the sweet and even neutral moments that we may have.

During this practice some of you noticed some painful experiences and emotions. Some of you needed to close for a little while. I am glad you allowed yourselves to practice emotional safety and take care of yourselves until you felt well enough to return to this practice. That was a wonderful way of creating emotional safety for yourselves.

Sometimes we need to shut down, sometimes we need to disconnect, sometimes we need to step away. There is no shame in that. It is a safety mechanism and a natural defense system, especially if we have spent our lives feeling unsafe. Learning to step away in order to find our sense of safety again can be a powerful and very useful tool.

When we are practicing emotional safety, we can ask ourselves, "What do I need right now?" Perhaps we may need some space or a break from what we are currently doing? Perhaps we need to feel safe in our relationship or friendship? Perhaps we need to be seen or heard by our partner, family member, or friend? Perhaps we desperately want to be understood, validated, and accepted? See if you can spend some time reflecting on your needs.

Superhero Training Steps:

Creating Safety: See if you can spend some time mindfully observing your physical and emotional needs, perhaps asking yourself some of the questions below. If you are able to support yourself in a few small ways, fantastic! If that is not possible right now and these steps do not seem realistic at this time, that's okay too. See if you can keep checking in with yourself until it is easier or more possible for you. See if you can respond to some of the prompts in your journal, noticing what you may need, stepping into your sanctuary (real or imaginary) any time you need. You can also download a PDF of the questions with space to record your answers at www.newharbinger.com/47520.

Evaluating Your Physical Safety: What do I need? Do I need to eat, drink some water, have some tea or coffee? Do I need to rest, sleep, or take a little break from what I am doing? Do I need to get away from a toxic or uncomfortable environment I am in, at least for a few minutes?

What can I do to provide that for myself, at least in some way?

Evaluating Your Emotional Safety: What do I need? Do I need a break? A hug? Reassurance? Do I need to breathe? To take a few minutes to play a game? Or to snuggle with my pet?

What can I do to provide that for myself, at least in some way?

Chapter 4

The Amulet of Vulnerability

I cannot remember how old I was when I started believing that stomachs were ugly. I must have been four. Overhearing my mother talk about her own stomach rang in my ears like a foghorn: stomachs are ugly.

I remember being five or six and sucking in my stomach whenever I would look in the mirror. The mirror became my self-imposed critic, scrutinizing every perceived imperfection, and the critical voice in my head became my abuser.

"Your stomach is ugly," it said. "And because of that, you will never be beautiful. And if you are not beautiful, then no one will marry you. And if no one will marry you, then you will die alone."

On most days, I used to suck it in. Some days, I used to punch it, as if physical abuse would help me shrink it. It didn't.

I ate. And I was afraid to eat. The scale at every doctor's office became my tormentor. Shortly after I got married, my gynecologist told me, "Be careful, after women get married, they gain weight. You don't want to do that."

He did not explain why that was an issue, only that I needed to make sure that it wasn't going to become one.

After my dear friend passed away from cancer, I went through one of the worst depression periods of my life. Along with the grief of losing her, all my previous unprocessed trauma that I was running away from caught up to me, knocking me down to my knees and rendering me unable to function. I feared for my life because living didn't seem like an option after a while. My doctor put me on an antidepressant, which in conjunction with therapy helped me to process my grief as well as the many previously unprocessed losses I was feeling in my stomach.

Some people lose weight when they are going through abuse, trauma, or grief, and other people gain weight when these events occur. For me, it was the latter. And although I started feeling better a few months after starting therapy and taking an antidepressant, my family was horrified about my weight gain. It did not matter that I was feeling better or that I was alive because of it. All I heard for the next two years was how fat I was, how I needed to lose weight: "What happened to you?" "Your husband won't keep being interested in you if you are so fat." "Have you tried dieting?"

All I kept thinking about every moment of every day was the size of my stomach. When I would look in the mirror, I would be horrified by what I saw. No matter what I was doing, in the back of my mind I was overwhelmed with the sensation of disgust toward myself. I hated taking pictures and would secretly un-tag myself from social media pictures that my friends posted of me, because as much as my family shamed me, I shamed myself more.

I would start exercise programs and I would quit after a few weeks because I hated them. I would try diets because I wanted so desperately to be thin, but I hated the food I was eating. I remember nearly choking on an egg-and-cucumber-only diet, hating every piece of it. The scale once again became my enemy—and not just the one at the doctor's office but the one in my house too. I used to joke that it liked to mess with me, that it somehow knew if I was "bad," because if I ever ate anything "unhealthy" or even thought about it, somehow I would have gained a pound or two on the scale.

My shame came from my experiences of being rejected and shamed about my weight. My self-shaming made me believe that I was unlovable and that I did not deserve compassion.

I hated myself. The idea that something about us is the reason why it is okay for people to judge and reject us can be the most damaging message we can receive. When we receive messages like these, we might internalize them, joining and amplifying the critical messages of others, and becoming our own tormentor.

Raise your hand if you have ever shamed yourself or worried that you would be rejected for the way you look.

"It's been that way all my life," Lisa says. "It doesn't matter how many degrees I have, how successful I am, how healthy or unhealthy I feel, or how happy I am. All that seems to matter to my family and the many people in my life is how much I weigh and whether or not I am fat."

"How has that affected you?" I ask her.

"In every way. I don't think there's a moment of my day in which I don't think about my weight," she says. "When I take the bus, I wonder what people think of me. If I stand, I worry that people will give me dirty looks or tell me I'm taking up too much space. If I sit because my feet are killing me from a long day, I worry that people will say or think that I am lazy. When I am eating a sandwich, people make comments. When I am eating a salad, people make comments. When I am exercising at the gym, people make comments. If I'm dating a thin man, he is praised as a hero for dating me. I could be cross-examining a witness in a grand jury trial and my thoughts are still about what people on the jury think about my weight and my outfit. People tell me to work out because they assume that I don't. But I've run eight marathons and did an Ironman triathlon last year. People assume that I eat nothing but junk food, but I don't, and I used to barely eat at all. There was one time I fainted because of not having enough food. Sometimes the message I seem to get is that 'it's better to be dead than to be fat.'"

"I completely understand that feeling where you're completely focused on that one thing about you that you have no control over," Victoria says. "I'm always worrying about whether or not I'm passing... you know... as a woman. In the mornings, I spend hours doing makeup and getting ready to leave. Sometimes I hate the way I look in the mirror. I always worry about whether people are judging me. Going to the restroom in public places is the most difficult experience for me. I never know if someone is going to ask me if I'm in the wrong bathroom, call the police, or yell at me or assault me. No matter what I am doing, in the back of my mind, I am wondering if people are judging me and if I am passing enough. Nothing hurts me more than when someone misgenders me. A waiter at a restaurant referred to me as 'sir' the other day. I just sat there. I didn't say or order anything. I just cried."

Sadly, both societal and individual transphobia and fat phobia can lead to shaming behaviors in the observers and shame feelings in the recipients of cruel comments or remarks. While some individuals may purposely wish to insult someone based on a particular feature (such as their gender identity, sexual orientation, or their weight), other individuals may not be aware how incredibly damaging their remarks, such as inquiries about one's diet and exercise, can be. Similar to racism, misogyny, ableism, ageism, and other forms of prejudice, transphobia and fat phobia can cut deep wounds in the survivors of these types of discrimination treatments.[8]

The messages that the perpetrators of prejudice deliberately or unintentionally send out to the recipients of their abuse are these:

- Because of this part of you (your skin color, race, gender identity, sexual orientation, culture, weight, etc.), you are not worthy of my respect
- Because of this part of you, you are not worthy of the same treatment as other people who do not have this feature
- This feature is bad
- You deserve to be shamed and mistreated because of this feature
- You brought this upon yourself
- Because of this part of you, you are not worthy of unconditional acceptance, love, and belonging

Ragen Chastain is an advocate, speaker, health coach, and athlete, and an expert in fat phobia. She writes that we live in a fat-phobic society, in which fat individuals are likely to be bullied, prejudiced against, stigmatized, and dehumanized (treated as less than human). She explains that fat individuals are less likely to receive the same job opportunities as thin people, are likely to experience bullying and rejection due to their weight, and are more likely to have doctors disregard their medical concerns. In her "Dances with Fat" blog, Ragen makes several recommendations for people whose doctors may disregard their presenting problems (used with permission)[9]:

1. In our limited time, I'd like to focus on (the presenting issue).
2. Do thin people ever come in for this issue (presenting problem)? What would you recommend for them?
3. Shame is bad for my health; I would ask you to first do no harm and provide me with shame-free healthcare.

Although many doctors consider their patients' health to be related to their body mass index (BMI), there is some controversy as to how indicative the BMI is regarding one's health status or prognosis. In fact, recent research studies describe the *obesity paradox*—a finding that overweight and obese individuals with cardiovascular diseases, as well as kidney disease, and autoimmune diseases, such as arthritis, appear to have a better prognosis compared to thin individuals with the same diagnoses.[10] Overall, the studies connected to the obesity paradox suggest that an individual's level of exercise is more predictive of their well-being than their weight or BMI number, and that the amount of one's exercise may not always lead to a change in one's weight.[11]

In an interview for this book, Chastain adds that although the word *fat* used to be applied as an insult, this word does not need to be feared or avoided: "Some individuals have unfortunately used the words 'gay' or 'queer' as insults as well, while these words in their literal meaning describe someone's sexual orientation. As both a fat and a queer person, I am hoping to take away the stigma attached to both of these words. The less we see them as insults, the more we can use them as neutral descriptors."

The group considers this for a moment. Tala speaks first.

"That word, *fat,* it's very hard for me. I used to be threatened with that word and shamed with that word. I don't know if I want to use it. I don't even like using the word *overweight.*"

"That's okay, Tala," I say to her. "Listen to your own needs. It's okay to use the words you identify with, and it's okay not to use the words that you find to be hurtful."

"For me it's the opposite," Lisa says. "I'm tired of being shamed for my body. It still hurts when people use this word to shame me, but I refuse to use it in a derogatory way. I am a fat woman. That's what I am. I've been shamed about it my entire life. But I'm done with that."

"How did that feel to say that?" I ask Lisa.

She smiles. "Empowering."

We have mentioned the emotion of shame a number of times so far. Let's differentiate between the emotions of *shame* and *guilt.* Brené Brown, a well-known vulnerability and shame researcher, says that *guilt* is specific to an action, such as missing an appointment or saying something that offended someone else.[12] On the other hand, *shame* means feeling bad about ourselves as a whole. Whereas guilt might lead us to think "*I did something bad,'* shame might lead us to think "*I am worthless.*"

Guilt can sometimes be helpful in that it can teach us which actions are helpful and which ones we should avoid in the future. On the other hand, shame tends to be ineffective. Shame is the leading mechanism in most mental health disorders, because when we fail to accept ourselves, we cannot possibly accept our symptoms. According to Brené Brown's research, shame can lead us to think that we are not good enough, unlovable, and are undeserving of love and belonging.[13]

Why is this so? Self-compassion researcher Chris Germer says that "Shame is an innocent emotion that arises from the wish to be loved."[14] What this means is that the emotion of shame shows up because we care. We care about connection. We care about being loved. We care about being a part of something, a part of someone's life. And some real or perceived aspect of our action, appearance, or culture may pose a real or perceived threat to this type of connection.

Hence, shame essentially arises out of rejection and fear of losing a meaningful connection. Interestingly, the opposite of our deepest fear, the inverse of our deepest shame, is our core human desire to be loved and accepted.

> I had six rounds of the strongest chemo. I then had seven weeks of radiation treatments. These were easy to do physically but harder mentally. All the doctors and techs were great, but it didn't stop the humiliation of having to expose myself to many strangers on a daily basis. The best thing I did for myself was going to a support group. I was skeptical and didn't know anyone. Those women took me under their wing and gave me so much info that I literally filled an entire notebook! They told me all my possible options, what to expect, what could possibly happen, and many coping strategies. I met with them through my entire process and after. I also learned that knowledge truly is power and that it is definitely okay to fight for what you believe in.
>
> —Amanda

"This is very hard," Tala says, her hands trembling. "We are talking about these thoughts of being worthless and not being good enough, and I am noticing that I have them all the time. I always worry that there will be a woman who is prettier or thinner than me whenever I go anywhere. When my boyfriend is with me, I always wonder if he would be better off with the person I think of as more attractive than me. I watch him to see if he is looking at other women. I don't believe him when he tells me that he doesn't. Then we fight and I think that he probably wants to leave me, and if he didn't want to leave me then, that he would want to leave me now. I am scared to go anywhere with him for the fear of seeing someone more attractive than me. And even if he's not with me, I still look at other women, wondering if he'd be better off with one of them."

"That's very courageous of you to notice that, Tala," I say to her. "I wonder if there may be a desire for some kind of emotional safety in those moments. If your boyfriend could tell you anything to support you, what would he say to you? What would you most want to hear from him?"

She looks down, deep in thought. After a few moments she looks up again. "I think... he would tell me that he loves me and only me. He would tell me that he is fully and completely happy with me and that I am the only one he wants to be with." She looks down again, shaking her head. "It's just... even if he said that, it would be really hard for me to believe that."

"Tala," I say to her as she looks up at me. "What would it be like for you to consider the possibility that you might be lovable—completely and utterly lovable and that you are already enough? What would that be like?"

She looks at me for a few moments and then tears begin to run down her face, as she lowers her head again. "I'm sorry. I don't know why I am crying."

"Sometimes when we lean into something vulnerable, such as a loving thought or a message, it can remind us of all the times that this particular need was not met. Some psychologists call this the **backdraft** effect.[15] Sometimes, it can be so overwhelming, that it can feel like we are on fire. It is perfectly okay to give ourselves the permission to open and close as much or as little as we need to."

She nods and then looks up at me. "I think I needed that. Thank you."

"Thank you for sharing that, Tala," Zaara says to her. "Hearing you, Lisa, and Victoria share your experiences today is making it easier for me to share mine." She takes a deep breath before she continues. "After the assault, I've become so afraid of being near men that I actually dropped a few courses taught by male instructors. Three years later, I still freeze when a man approaches me to ask me a question on campus." Another breath. "I have recently started dating again. My boyfriend is very nice and patient. We are talking about getting married one day. He doesn't know about the assault. I am scared of what will happen when we get married. I am scared that when we are going to have sex, he won't want to be with me. I am scared that he will not understand what I went through. I am scared of how I might react when we are intimate. And I don't even know if I can." She breathes through her tears, as the rest of us breathe with her, giving her space and safety to process how she is feeling. After a minute, she nods that she is ready to continue.

Divya raises her hand to go next. "I can relate to what you are saying, Zaara. I may never have been assaulted but I really struggle being intimate with my husband. He doesn't understand how much pain I am in. I am in pain every day. Some days, my pain is intolerable. Some days I can barely move.

"He gets upset if I don't want to be intimate with him. Sometimes it hurts so much that I ask him to stop. He does but he doesn't always understand. He doesn't see my pain, and when he sees me moving about, he assumes that I am more able to function than I actually am. He blames everything on my school and wants me to quit my course. But the truth is that it's making me happy. Ever since I became a mom, my depression worsened. Don't get me wrong. I love my children and I love my time with them. But the truth is that I am always tired. I am always overwhelmed. It feels like I am always *on*. I cry when no one is watching. I cry in the shower. I am lonely but I am never alone. I am busy without any scheduled breaks. I'm just so tired. And it might seem strange but the last thing I want to do is to quit school."

"Thank you so much for sharing that, Divya. A lot of stay-at-home moms report experiences similar to yours. When we work at home or from home, we may not allow ourselves the permission to rest. We may not be able to leave our work at work. And I can see how important being in school is to you. If I may ask, what does it function to do?"

She thinks about it. "I guess it allows me to use my mind in a different way. I'm studying architecture. I really like it because it's like a puzzle to me. Sometimes it's frustrating but it's also very rewarding to be able to figure it out."

"And how is your pain when you are working on your architecture projects?"

"Sometimes it's worse, such as when I've been sitting at my table working on my homework for too long."

"And at other times?"

"At other times it's better. At times when I am deeply engrossed in my project, I hardly notice it."

"And how do you feel then?" I ask her.

She smiles. "Happy. Like this is what I am meant to be doing."

When we feel connected to our sense of purpose, we are likely to feel more empowered. However, sometimes our own shame experiences may get in the way of us making such meaningful connections. In order for us to learn to manage shame, we need to understand it. We all experience shame. In fact, most of us experience shame in the same way: by believing that we are not good enough at something that means a lot to us. At its core, shame is usually tied to something we really care about. The inverse of our shame, fear, and pain are the root of our core values. Our heart hurts because it's supposed to. Our heart hurts because it's trying to tell us how important a particular person or event is. In understanding this pain, we can uncover our greatest strength and learn to connect with our passions instead of running away from them.

For example, people who care about their relationship may believe that they are not a good partner, and people who care about being a parent may believe that they are a terrible parent. Psychologist Marsha Linehan specializes in helping people with borderline personality disorder, a mental health disorder which is known for people's struggle with shame, fear of getting rejected, and difficulty experiencing painful emotions. Linehan says that the function of shame is to protect us from getting rejected. We might be so afraid of getting rejected from our support system or group that we may hide who we are from them.[16]

Over time, running away from shame may not only preclude us from opening up to others, but it may also preclude us from opening up to ourselves. Running away from shame occurs because we do not want to feel it, but paradoxically the opposite happens: the more we attempt to run away from shame, the more we might experience it. There are probably parts of ourselves that we may know about but refuse to acknowledge for the fear of being found out, or perhaps even for the fear of self-rejection. Self-rejection is a real phenomenon, and when we reject ourselves, when we are at the pit of our shame, we might shut down. Some individuals may stop talking or moving, sometimes feeling paralyzed when they are deep within the trauma of their shame response. Shame can sometimes function as a self-punishment for something that isn't our responsibility. For example, it is not uncommon for adult survivors of childhood sexual trauma to feel shame about having been abused.

People experiencing shame (for example, after being yelled at by a family member or a significant other) will usually lower their head, sometimes losing color in their face. Sometimes they might cry. Other times, they may seem paralyzed. This shutdown is the body's attempt to escape the pain. Unfortunately, many people witnessing the shutdown may not understand what is happening and may proceed to further shame the individual, frustrated at the apparent lack of verbal response or eye contact. The person yelling may be actively trying to establish a bond, frustrated with the lack of interaction, while the person shutting down may be attempting to escape the excruciating pain that they are feeling. Hurt people hurt people. They may hurt people unintentionally, but they do. And healed people heal people with compassion and understanding.

"I can relate to that statement—*hurt people hurt people*," Hannah says. "I notice that when I have my OCD thoughts about hurting my daughter, I start shaming myself for being a bad mom. When my husband asks me why I can't change her diaper, instead of explaining to him what I am going through, I lash out and we end up fighting, and I end up feeling even worse. Now, in addition to feeling like a terrible mom, I also feel like a terrible wife."

"Thank you so much for sharing your experience with us, Hannah," I say to her. "If you could possibly tell your husband what is going on for you at that time, what would you say to him?"

She sighs. "I would tell him that my heart breaks every day when I see my baby and I can't seem to find the courage to pick her up. I would tell him that I constantly shame myself, thinking that I am a bad mom to her and a bad partner to him. I would tell him that I wish I would just be able to find the strength to connect with my family but that it's really hard right now. I would tell him that I just wish he knew how much I love them both and how hard I am trying. Every day. All the time. I don't want this nightmare anymore. I didn't ask for this. And I would do anything to make it stop."

She breathes for a while, her hands squeezing together, tears running down her face. We breathe with her, sharing her pain, holding a safe space for her. Isabella hands her a tissue. After a few moments, Hannah blows her nose and nods that she is ready to continue.

"Vulnerability is both the most terrifying and also the most courageous thing of which we are capable." I say. "We fear vulnerability because it has the potential to expose our raw, naked, flawed self to the world. And at the root of that vulnerability is the most lovable part of ourselves."

"I really struggle with that part," Isabella says. "The part about opening up about my vulnerability."

"Me too," Victoria says.

"Me too," Lisa, Tala, and Zaara say.

"I've always struggled with organization," Isabella continues. "My parents always used to say that I am unfocused. Things that other people can do in ten minutes may take me a few hours. I get distracted. I am always late to my appointments. I am interested in so many things but it's hard for me to stay committed to any of them. People tell me to keep lists. And I do, but I may forget to write something down or get distracted as I am writing something down. My ex left me because she said I was too 'all over the place.' Sometimes I wonder if me getting cancer is a punishment for being 'all over the place,' as she put it. I don't know how to change it. I've never been able to."

There is an assumption that we are all supposed to fit in to some kind of a universal box. But in reality, we are all a work of art. The beauty of art is that it is diverse and eclectic. You aren't meant to fit into a box because you are a rainbow, and rainbows don't belong in boxes. What may seem like disorganization to some may seem like art to others. You may not fall within the template that others have designed for you, but it doesn't mean that you have to, and it doesn't mean that your way is the wrong way.

In working on recovering from shame, the first step is to name it. Brené Brown says that the less we talk about shame, the more we feel it, and the more we talk about it, the less we feel it.[17] Hence, the first step is to externalize shame—to name it, look at it, study it, notice it. Then, we can examine ways to heal *with* it (not *from* it).

I surveyed more than three hundred women to consider what kinds of emotional triggers and vulnerabilities may come up for them. Here is a list of their responses, which is by no means fully comprehensive, but it is a good starting point. Take a look at this list and see if any of these triggers or vulnerabilities have ever come up for you:

Asking my partner how I look	When someone makes a reference to my physical appearance, even if it's a compliment
When men punch other things around me or act aggressively	When a male boss sits on their desk in front of me, towering over me, and spreading their legs. They may not realize it, but it's triggering
Stonewalling during discussions	A condescending tone
Someone saying that I am "being too sensitive" when I have a legitimate concern	People explaining something to me that I know a lot about
Someone telling me that my words mean something different than what they actually do	Sexism in the workplace, especially from other women
Telling someone that I am in pain	People forcing me to smile
Someone repeatedly speaking over me during a conversation	When people ask me if I'm okay. I'm never okay but I'm too scared to say that
A male coworker putting his arm around my waist	When someone approaches me at night when I'm walking alone
A male massage therapist not draping me	Going to a multistory parking garage by myself

Women perceiving me as a threat because of my gender	When someone talks to my husband as if my husband speaks for me
Someone looking through my phone without asking	Being alone in a stairwell or elevator with a strange man
Going to the beach or swimming pool	Men coming up to my car
People gossiping about my divorce	Someone putting a hand over my mouth, even in a playful manner
When someone tries to convince me I hadn't given "us" enough of a chance after I said no	Men yelling around me
A stranger or someone who likes me showing up at my house	As a teenager working as a waitress on a holiday
Someone I dated showing up at my work	Men grabbing my arms to look at my tattoos or coming too close to look at them without permission
Choosing to keep my maiden name after marriage	Comments that question my sexuality
Talking about my mental illness	When I get treated like trash for turning down a man's advances
Starting a relationship	Ending a relationship
Having a child	Losing a child
Being a stay-at-home mom	Being a working mom
Earning more than my partner	Earning less than my partner
Talking about money, sex, and intimacy	Explaining why something triggered me

Someone towering over me	When there is a woman who I think is prettier than I am
Someone standing too close to me	Feeling hungry
Being asked about or commented on my weight or food	Being recommended a diet or exercise plan
Seeing before and after pictures	Reading about people's "successful" weight-loss journeys
Being told that what happened to me "wasn't that bad"	When people are eating around me
Medical exams/breast exams	When I am the only fat person in the room
Gynecological exams	Making eye contact
Not being given privacy to change at the doctor's office	Being accepted, loved, and understood
Anyone grabbing my wrists or ankles	Being naked in front of a mirror
Breastfeeding or lactating in public	Being naked in front of my partner
Having my arms held to my sides or anything that limits my body autonomy	Passing as my gender or my gender being questioned, being misgendered
Being referred to as a "girl" instead of "woman"	Going to the bathroom
My exit path being blocked in any way	Someone testing my geek credibility (how much I know about a comic, game, or sport)
If someone walks too closely behind me	Having to explain my pain/physical condition to someone

Were there any situations that you could relate to? Did you notice a change in your own emotions as you were reviewing this table? Sometimes we might feel sad, angry, anxious, or full of many different emotions in response to a trigger. All emotions are allowed. All emotions are okay. They are all necessary and they are all informative in terms of our present needs.

Whenever we are presented with something that makes us feel ashamed or vulnerable, we might shut down and withdraw, or we might connect with it and work toward healing it.[18] If we shut down, it does not mean that we are doing something wrong, nor does it mean that we are at fault for this reaction. It simply means that in that moment we may not have enough resources to manage the pain that is arising for us. The practice of acknowledging shame and vulnerability emotions is exactly that—a *practice*. And that means that you cannot get it wrong. In trying it out, you are already succeeding. The success is not in the outcome (how you are feeling at the end), it is in the *action* of noting and exploring your current experiences.

Although we primarily talked about vulnerability as consisting of emotions such as shame and anxiety, vulnerability also includes other emotions, such as joy. Brené Brown suggests that many people may engage in *foreboding joy*—fearing and being apprehensive about experiencing this emotion.[19] Brown finds that some people may be anxious to acknowledge it when they experience joy because they might be afraid that if they do, something awful might happen to take it all away from them. And although always being on the lookout for any negative outcome may seem protective, it actually does not allow us to savor the wonderful things that may be showing up in our life.

"That's definitely true for me," Hannah says. "I am always on the lookout for something to go wrong."

"So, is it fair to say that overall, when things are going well or when things are neutral, you're more likely to be anxious and overwhelmed?" I ask.

"Yes, exactly."

"How about when there's a crisis?"

"You know, it's funny, but it seems like that's about the only time my anxiety is down. I am always on the lookout for a crisis, and when it actually happens I have almost no anxiety until it passes."

No mud, no lotus.

I smile at her. "It seems you've discovered your superpower. You are a warrior. Always ready to protect others."

She smiles back.

As odd as it may seem, your vulnerability is your greatest strength. It is your magic amulet and your heart is your superpower. There is an expression I like: "No mud, no lotus." What it means to me is that the most beautiful things in the world are ones that blossom in muddy circumstances. Perhaps it is that mud that makes the lotus whole and more beautiful.

Every person has the right to pursue their happiness. Women do not need to be forced into perfection—we already are perfect. And that means that every one of you, with every part of you, with every moment of darkness, with every smile and every tear, is perfect. This does not mean that we are not flawed. We are. As are all humans. And it is *because* of our flaws, not despite them, that we are perfect. Perfectly human. Perfectly worthy of unconditional love. Just the way we are. And whether you are the kind of woman who gets married, divorced, or doesn't ever want to get married, whether you are one to have children, or to choose not to have children, or are unable to, whether you are a career woman, a freelancer, a CEO, a working mom, or a stay-at-home mom, whichever way you look, feel, and function, there are no conditions you have to meet and there is nothing you have to do or to hide. You've already earned it. You are already worth it. You are already loved. You are already a perfect woman.

Superhero Training Step: If and when you feel comfortable, please write down in your journal some of the aspects in your life that make you feel vulnerable. Are there thoughts that you are struggling with, such as I am not smart/attractive/thin/successful enough, or fears of being found out if people really got to know you? Given these vulnerabilities, what might be some of your emotional needs—to be loved, noticed, understood, accepted, supported?

Take as much time as you need with this practice. At any point, if you need to take a breath or a break, give yourself the permission to do so.

Chapter 5

The Magic of Connection

You might recall our superheroing model:

Superheroing = connection + safety

We've been working on emotional safety and will continue to do so throughout the book. And now, we will also turn our attention to establishing a sense of *connection*. Connection is any kind of physical, emotional, or sometimes spiritual contact with what we hold dear to us, including our loved ones, our core values, and, as difficult as it may be sometimes, ourselves. It means prioritizing meaningful contact with meaningful beings and activities in our lives.

This chapter will focus on establishing connection with others, whereas chapters 6 and 7 will focus on establishing a sense of connection with ourselves, and chapters 8 to 10 will focus on creating a sense of purpose and becoming a superhero in real life (IRL).

Establishing a sense of connection with others can be anything from texting a loved one to petting your dog or cat to cuddling with someone. After meeting our basic survival needs for food, water, sleep, and physiological safety (safety from physical danger), connection is the next most important mechanism of survival. It can help us find the courage to navigate difficult experiences and feel more able to manage them. On the other hand, disconnection can feel not only emotionally painful but even physically painful. Emotional rejection, similar to physical injury, can produce an activation in the pain regions of our brain, whereas emotional connection and receiving support from our loved ones can actually soothe this response.

When I was twenty-one, I worked as a research assistant in a hospital in New York City. One day, while rushing down the stairs at work, I slipped and fell, hitting my head. Being in the hospital, I went into the emergency room as soon as I was able to walk. The emergency room neurologist I saw confirmed that I had a concussion, and I was ordered to rest and refrain from screens and stress.

I called my (then) partner to pick me up and take me home. Let's call him "Jim." That night, Jim and I were supposed to go to a premiere of a film we had been anticipating for over six months. When learning about my concussion, he expressed his sympathy but proceeded to say that it made no sense for both of us to miss the film and that him being with me would not take away my concussion nor my physical pain. He suggested I take a taxi home and that he should go see the film without me.

I remember feeling really torn. On the one hand, I thought Jim had a point, logically speaking. If he came to be with me and missed the film, we would both miss out. But on the other hand, I couldn't help but feel rejected and angry that Jim chose to see a movie over picking me up from the hospital and spending time with me after I got injured. I ended up having to take the subway home by myself after being discharged from the emergency room. I couldn't figure out why it bothered me as much as it did that Jim wasn't there for me. I kept shaming myself, thinking that I was being too needy, or even "crazy" for wanting Jim to drop his plans to be with me.

Years later, I realized that my needs were not wrong. Research studies actually show that emotional support and/or gentle touch, such as holding someone's hand during a painful procedure, actually reduces the physical perception and the emotional distress that comes with that painful experience. Furthermore, evidence shows that receiving physical support from our loved one, such as hand-holding, produces significantly larger pain-reduction effects than holding the hand of a stranger (for example, a nurse), but that both can help reduce the effects of physical and emotional pain.[20]

Both giving and receiving emotional support have been shown to improve physical and psychological health and are even believed to prolong our lifespan.[21] A few studies find that loved ones' support can lead to significant improvements in physical health when it comes to blood pressure regulation,[22] diabetes, and heart disease,[23] and may play a role in reducing the spread of certain types of cancer.[24]

This means that when we are asking our loved ones to support us through a difficult moment, we are not "needy," we are in survival mode. And if it feels like you're dying when your loved one is not being compassionate or supportive, you are not being "dramatic," your feelings are legitimate and valid. Just as no one would call you "needy" for screaming for help when you are literally drowning in the river, you are also just as justified in asking for help when you are drowning in the ocean of immense emotional or physical pain. The experience of emotional or physical pain is already painful enough as it is, and hence our loved ones' refusal to support us might feel excruciating. It is at times like these, times when we may not feel as if anyone can support us, understand us, or hold our hand through an overwhelming experience, that we might feel most alone and struggle in coping with the present situation. Oftentimes, it is not the event itself that may make it hard for people to cope with it, it is the lack of adequate support to get us through it that can make the experience seem unmanageable. Sometimes, we feel most lonely when we are with a loved one or a group of friends, all of whom "just don't get it." In fact, when we are already struggling, feeling disconnected can make us feel more alone than if we were not to be around others.

Why does it work this way? From birth, humans are meant to have warm, supportive interactions with their parents or other caretakers. As children, we need to be picked up and comforted just as much as we need to be fed. A groundbreaking study by researcher Harry Harlow in 1959 supports this notion. In the study, investigators removed infant monkeys from their mothers at a young age. When the infant monkeys were taken out of their cages, they were presented with two fake mother monkey models: one was a wire model, which provided the infants with milk, and the other was a soft cloth model, almost like a stuffed animal. When let out of their cages, the infant monkeys would spend a few minutes feeding from the wire monkey model and then would spend most of their other time cuddling the cloth monkey. In addition, when they were frightened (for example, by a loud noise), the infant monkeys ran toward the cloth monkey, not toward the wire model.[25] This study, along with many others, demonstrates the need for creating a safe sense of connection for children with their caretakers.[26]

But what about adults? Research studies find that adults need a sense of connection in their relationships similar to how children do and that it is directly related to relationship satisfaction. Another word for creating a sense of connection with others is *attachment.*[27] Attachment researchers have uncovered four different attachment styles: anxious, avoidant, secure, and anxious-avoidant (sometimes referred to as "disorganized").[28] For the purposes of this book, we will primarily focus on the first three attachment styles. These styles can be thought of as different languages, different ways that people express their needs and respond to other people's needs.

Have you ever been told any of the following?

- "You are too needy."
- "You are too insecure."
- "You are crazy."
- "You are too sensitive."
- "Just forget about it."
- "You need to let it go."
- "I don't want to talk about it."
- "I said I was sorry, what more do you want?"

Have any of you experienced these?

"Yes. All of them," Isabella says, sighing. "My parents always said that I was 'too emotional' and 'crazy.' Most of my exes told me that I was irrational in how I felt. One of my exes yelled at me for crying when she refused to take me to my first chemo infusion. She yelled that it made no sense for her to miss an important meeting at work 'just to sit and do nothing' with me. My cancer was in my breast, but when she said that, I felt it in my heart. I knew that her being there wouldn't take the cancer away, but I couldn't explain to her how much I needed her there. In the end, I ended up apologizing and going alone anyway. I cried the entire time."

Most people who are criticized about their emotional support needs might end up feeling ashamed about feeling "too dependent" on their partner and friends. However, in reality, there is nothing wrong with having these needs. These needs are legitimate and important. What it might mean sometimes, however, is that the particular person who expressed such critical feedback about our own needs may have a different understanding of how connection works and might have different connection needs. Sometimes, our own parents, friends, partners, and siblings may have completely different needs from us. None of those needs is wrong. It's like having different hair or eye color. All are acceptable; they are just different.

If you'd like to learn more about different attachment styles and how they can affect your romantic relationships, I highly recommend the book *Attached,* by psychiatrist and neuroscientist Dr. Amir Levine and consultant and trainer Rachel Heller.[29]

Let's briefly review the three previously mentioned attachment types:

Anxious attachment type

People with this attachment type crave intimacy with loved ones and are highly sensitive to rejection. If this is your attachment style, you may worry that your loved ones may not like you or will reject you if they *really* get to know you. You might anticipate not having your needs met and assume that your loved ones are angry with you or do not want to be around you. As a result, you might either lash out, regretting it later, or suppress your own needs, not wanting to upset your loved ones, only to feel resentful toward them later. Some individuals with this attachment type may prefer the intimacy of one or two friends over larger but less personal groups. Individuals with this attachment type are likely not to get their needs met if they are attempting to connect with an individual with an avoidant attachment type but are likely to get their needs met from someone with a secure attachment type.[30][31]

Avoidant attachment type

People with this attachment type value independence and may struggle with intimacy. For some individuals with this attachment style, intimacy and emotional closeness may feel as if they are giving up their sense of autonomy or a part of themselves. If this is your attachment style, you might struggle with committing to a partner or plans, or you may have rigid expectations in what makes a perfect partner or friend, and if these are not met, you may be likely to run. You might be unwilling to change some of your routines because it might feel suffocating or unfair to you. You might be afraid of getting hurt and therefore might be the first to end a relationship or a friendship and might "ghost" someone (stop communicating with someone without an explanation) if you're feeling uncomfortable with telling them how you feel.

Some individuals with this attachment type may also struggle with fidelity and may have many friends but few close friends. They might be likable and charismatic but might struggle to fully open up to anyone. Some individuals with this attachment type may struggle with empathy toward their romantic partners or other people closest to them but may be able to empathize with other people, such as colleagues and acquaintances. Some anxious and avoidant partnerships bring out the worst in each other because they may inadvertently be each other's triggers, with anxious-type individuals pulling for more closeness and with avoidant-type individuals wanting more space and independence.[3233]

Secure attachment type

Individuals with this attachment type tend to be compassionate and responsive to their partner's needs. They believe that they are worthy of love and belonging, and they are also likely to be most open and vulnerable in their communication style. They don't worry about their loved ones' feelings for them as much as the individuals with an anxious attachment type do and are more responsive to their loved ones' needs than individuals with an avoidant attachment type. In general, individuals with this attachment type are likely to get along with individuals of all attachment types. Individuals with secure attachment type are typically more even keeled and may sometimes be rejected by individuals with an anxious attachment style because they may not cause as much anxiety to their partners as individuals with avoidant attachment styles do (anxiety hyperarousal is sometimes mistaken for love).

Tala shakes her head. "Wow. I'm realizing that my attachment style is *anxious* and most of the people I've dated were *avoidant* in their attachment style. Why do I do that to myself? Why do I keep on picking men who aren't right for me?"

I smile at her. "This might sound strange, but many people with anxious attachment style go through the exact same experience."

It's not you, it's stats

There is nothing wrong with you if you feel that you have connected with people with an attachment style opposite from yours. There are more of them! According to attachment researchers, there are more people with avoidant attachment style in the dating pool, as well as friendship pool, because they are more likely to jump from partner to partner, or from one friend to another friend.[34]

In addition, we tend to gravitate toward that which is familiar to us. Hence, we might be likely to repeat our old patterns. People with an anxious attachment style and people with an avoidant attachment style may often feel a strong spark in the beginning stages of their relationship. Sometimes, when both parties are aware of each other's needs, they can support each other, in that a person with an avoidant attachment type may learn to recognize their loved one's needs and reassure them while a person with an anxious attachment style may over time learn that their partner may value independence and that this need does not mean that their partner does not want to be with them.

In this case, both people may go on to develop a secure sense of attachment with one another over time. However, at other times, people with an anxious attachment style may need support or reassurance, which sometimes may lead the person with an avoidant attachment style to feel annoyed or distant, refusing to give in or compromise. This, in turn, can lead to the person with an anxious attachment style to feel rejected and, sometimes, traumatized, especially if they have a history of emotional abuse or rejection already. In fact, people with a history of rejection are likely to be more sensitive to negative emotional experiences. Furthermore, the more they try to suppress or "just don't feel" their emotions, the more likely they are to feel depressed.[35]

"But how do you explain this to someone?" Victoria asks. "I've always been told to wait at least three days before calling someone after a date and never to be the first person to say, 'I love you.' I feel exhausted by these games, but I don't ever want to scare the person I'm dating."

"You bring up a great point, Victoria," I tell her. "Most of us have been taught to play hard to get and to pretend not to be interested in the person we are dating. Unfortunately, when we act this way, we are sending mixed messages to our partner or perhaps our friends, as this rule applies to all close relationships. By pretending that we want independence, or a low amount of communication or support, that is exactly what we are likely to receive. In that case, we might feel both rejected and resentful. When this occurs, our very attempt to become close to a loved one can backfire. On the other hand, if what we truly crave is closeness, communication, and connection, we also have the right to ask for that directly and honestly.

"It is okay to let someone know right away that you may be someone who likes to communicate at least once a day, or that you like to spend quality time with your partner or friend. If that is what you want, ask for it. If you get it, great! If not, then perhaps this will not be the right person to support you in this way. It makes you seem honest and can make you more likely to get what you want."

"I want that," Isabella says. "I want to receive support from my current partner and my friends. But in the past, I've been told that I'm too dependent, so I try to just do everything myself now."

"Me too," Victoria agrees.

The toxicity of dependency shaming

For years, child experts used to tell parents to let their babies cry themselves to sleep, not to coddle them, not to soothe them when they are in distress. However, research studies conducted over the past few decades show that too much emotional deprivation can negatively affect our physical and psychological health. Emotional abuse and neglect in childhood, such as that seen in some children who are abandoned at an early age, can actually lead to depression, anxiety, and PTSD in adulthood.[36] Severe cases of emotional abuse and neglect can actually change someone's brain structure by reducing the volume (a.k.a. *gray matter*) of neurons (brain cells) that a person has and can even resemble the brain activity of people with epilepsy.[37] This means that, as humans, we actually need emotional support to thrive and function.

Sadly, the experiences of being shamed for being vulnerable, for having a basic human need for connection and support, can make us feel emotionally unsafe in asking for the very kind of help that we may really need. One way to manage this is to evaluate the kind of connections that you would want. For example, if you would want someone to give you a hug when you've had a rough day, reassure you, or just listen to you without giving you advice or trying to change your mind, you have the right to ask for that.

Your needs are perfectly okay and perfectly allowed.

> I remember sitting in a car with my mother. She said, "Don't ever have children. They put your life on hold, and frankly I wish I never had kids."
>
> "Was I a mistake?"
>
> She instantly replied, "Yes."
>
> I don't remember much of the conversation after that, but I remember I had looked out the window and silently cried.
>
> In July 2017, I ended my relationship with my mother. That moment has shaped me into who I am and where I am at this moment. I strive to be the best I can be. I strive to show everyone love and kindness, and to make sure they know that I love them and care for them.
>
> It's okay to feel the way you do. I still hurt to this day, but as I was once told, family isn't blood. It's the people who love you and care for you as you are. You aren't alone, and I will be there for you, and I believe that everything will work out. You don't have to follow the plan that was laid before you. You can do anything. I believe in you.
>
> —Thesally

What kind of connection do you want?

To evaluate what you need, see if any of these prompt you to consider what kind of a connection you may need when you are struggling.

When I am feeling sad/angry/anxious, what would be most helpful is if my partner/friend/family member would...

- Give me a hug
- Listen attentively without interrupting and without giving advice
- Let me vent about it
- Hold my hand or rub my back
- Bring me food or a hot beverage
- Give me advice on how to fix it
- Make time for me
- Bring me a small gift or a card to let me know they're thinking about me
- Understand that I may need my space and alone time to process things
- Reassure me that everything is going to be okay or that things will get better
- Tell me that they understand what I am going through and how difficult it is for me right now
- Provide a distraction for me—take me to the movies or show me a funny video

Looking at these types of connecting with others, what kind of connection would you want?

"For me, I find that it's most helpful when my husband listens to me without giving me advice, holds my hand and tells me that he understands how hard it is for me to go through all the pain I'm going through," Divya says. "Usually, he is very resistant to that. If I start telling him how I feel, he usually starts giving me advice on how I should fix it. Then I tell him it's not helpful and that I just need him to listen to me. Then he gets mad at me and we fight. But last night, he actually listened and supported me."

"That's wonderful, Divya," I tell her. "I'm glad he was able to be there for you and I am glad you are identifying what you need when you are having a rough time. What was different last night that allowed you both to connect in this way?"

"Usually, I start telling him how I feel and then he immediately tries to 'fix' me."

"And last night?" I ask her.

"Last night, I told him that I was going to tell him how I feel and that I would like for him to hold my hand and to just listen. I told him it would help me. It was very vulnerable, but I wanted to try it."

"And then what happened?"

"He sat with me and said, 'OK.' He held my hand. I told him how I felt. He didn't interrupt me. He just looked at me and held my hand when I was talking. He then asked me if it was helpful for him to listen to me and if he could do anything else for me. For some reason, just him saying that made me feel even better. I was still in pain, but I wasn't so bothered by it. Not like I usually am."

"How did you feel?"

"Loved. I felt like he truly loves me and understands me. I felt close to him. We ended up being intimate. It was nice."

"See, for me, it's the opposite," Lisa says. "When I am upset, I just want to have my own space. I want to process what's going on. I sometimes want to go on a walk or spend time with my dog. Usually though, I dive into my work because when I am working I feel more empowered, like I'm making a difference, you know? So, if someone hurts my feelings or when I am going through a breakup, I usually work more than usual."

"I'm glad you're able to identify ways in which you feel more connected to your core values—through work. And it seems like your ability to help others keeps you going even when you are having a rough time yourself."

She nods. "Exactly. Don't get me wrong, I enjoy relationships, but I also value my alone time. I value my independence, my training, and my career. I feel most connected when I am walking, running, hiking, or working. It's easier for me to connect to my work and exercise than to other people."

"That's great, Lisa. I'm glad you are able to find connection in this way and identify actions and environments that nourish you."

Everyone has different preferences and different ideas of what they want and what they don't want. No matter how much you may agree or disagree with someone else, everyone deserves to be treated with respect. We may not always fully understand another person when all we can see are their surface-level actions. Similarly, we may not always understand our own needs and preferences when we are only aware of our surface-level experiences. Diving deeper into understanding our own connection needs and preferences, let's look at the iceberg model of connection.

Iceberg model of connection

What we see above the water, the tip of the iceberg, are our immediate thoughts, feelings, and actions. What we may not see, the depth of the iceberg, are our core needs for connection, acceptance, love, and understanding. On the surface, we may be fighting off anxiety, depression, and trying to run away from our feelings. At the core of the iceberg, we are fighting for connection. And if connection is at the core of what it's all about, then perhaps the focus needs to be not on what we don't want (painful emotions and experiences) but on what we *do* want (love, belonging, making a difference).

When our core needs are not met, we are likely to rebel, whether it is by fighting, running away/threatening to run away, or shutting down. However, when our needs are met, we may feel physically and emotionally stronger and more solid in our foundation. In fact, regardless of our attachment styles, when we are able to receive consistent support for our needs from a loved one, such as a partner, a friend, a family member, or a pet, we are likely to experience a secure attachment to that living being. Interestingly, being able to receive such secure and reliable support from a loved one can increase independence and can give us the courage to take bigger steps in our own lives.[38]

It's not about the socks

Most people who fight with their loved ones start off fighting about something that seems trivial, such as not picking up their dirty socks off the floor. They may get into a fight about socks, one accusing the other of *never* picking up after themselves, while the other may get defensive or distant: "Here we go again, you're *always* nagging." The fight might then evolve into other topics, such as what happened at the picnic last year, about a forgotten birthday, a broken promise, and then a fight about how many fights there have been. It's enough to make anyone's head spin. We might feel light-headed, frustrated, angry, confused, and just wanting to be heard, while also wanting the fighting to stop.

Fights like these are not about the socks on the floor. They're nearly always about the core of the iceberg—our unmet needs and emotional desires. What we say when we are frustrated and what is underneath the surface are usually two completely different things.

Here's an example: the two monsters that follow are seemingly arguing about one's critical patterns and the other's seeming lack of concern. These surface communication patterns make it seem as though they abhor each other. However, when we examine their thought bubbles, we see that they care for each other and worry about how their partner feels about them.

What these two monsters are verbally communicating and what they actually need are two different things. It's not about the forgotten chores, it's about feeling supported, respected, cared for, needed and, most importantly, loved. We care! We care so much that it hurts. We care so much that our heart bleeds. That is why we fight. We are fighting for connection. And if in those moments those very needs were to be communicated, the argument may change.

When do these types of arguments come up? They might come up when our own resources are running low—when we are hungry, tired, burned out, worried about our finances or about our relationship, when we are ill or when the weather changes, when we are triggered, or when we feel bad about ourselves. In other words, conflicts are most likely to arise at the time when we (and/or our loved one) have unmet needs.

Fighting then becomes a survival mechanism. It's not wrong to fight. And it's *how* we fight that's important.

If conflicts occur often, it may be important to recognize the surface mechanisms (thoughts, feelings, and behaviors), as well as the core emotional needs, which tend to arise in most arguments. It may also be worthwhile to examine the typical resistance behaviors that often come up in arguments. These include:

- Yelling
- Criticizing
- Shaming
- Threatening to leave
- Playing games or trying to even the score (for example, not calling someone out of spite)
- Hurting yourself (emotionally or physically)
- Shutting down

All of these behaviors are completely understandable. When we engage in these, we are trying to survive, to be heard and validated. However, these behaviors may actually harm you and harm your relationship with your loved ones in the long term. So, if the goal is to have our needs met, then we can look at strategies to maximize those outcomes.

When we are presented with a painful situation in which our needs are not being met, it can be helpful to reflect on what is showing up for us at the tip of our iceberg (our thoughts, feelings, and behaviors), as well as what these may indicate about our needs at the core of our iceberg. Once we are able to figure out what we need, we might be able to ask for it directly from our loved ones.

It is perfectly okay to ask for support. It does not make you needy, it does not make you a burden, it makes you human.

There are different ways of asking for what you need: there is connection communication, and disconnection communication. *Disconnection communication* is critical, punishing, and/or avoidant. It includes passive, aggressive, and passive-aggressive communication styles. Although at the core of it is the desire for connection, this type of communication usually intensifies conflicts and makes it less likely that our needs will be met. On the other hand, *connection communication* tends to be honest, vulnerable, and assertive.

Let's break these down.

Disconnection communication:

Passive: not telling others what you need and just going along with what others decide to do. For example, you invite your friend to hang out when you are struggling with depression. Your friend says that they are busy. You do not specify what you are going through because they are "too busy for you anyway." This passive type of communication can create disconnection in any relationship because it doesn't allow others to know what your needs are, and therefore it does not allow them a chance to meet your needs. In addition, passive communication often creates resentment because we might believe that if people truly cared, they would just know that they need to reach out and support us.

Aggressive: yelling at others, criticizing, or threatening others to meet your needs. For example, threatening your partner that you will leave them if they are not available to support you. This style of communication might initially get your needs met but might lead to further conflicts and resentment in the future, often leading to more disconnection in communication.

Passive-aggressive: pretending to be passive or agreeable while being resistant at the same time. Examples of passive-aggressive communication include using sarcasm, using indirect ways to make someone feel bad about themselves (for example, "Thank you for this present, it must have taken you all of two minutes to pick it out"). Other examples of passive-aggressive communication include using silence or rejection as punishment, verbally stating "I'm fine" or "I don't care" when the tone implies the opposite, as well as disguised criticism (such as "I don't mean to be critical but..."). These types of communication styles can be frustrating for all involved parties because they do not clearly communicate what someone's needs are and how they can be met, creating resentment and confusion.

Other examples of disconnection communication:

1) "You never/always do this": Using "always" or "never" terms can make another person feel and act in a defensive way and is more likely to lead to disconnection. Instead, consider using specific examples, such as, "Last week when you were late to our meeting, it hurt my feelings."

2) "YOU hurt me": Using the "you" language in a fight can feel "finger-pointy" and critical. Instead, consider using "I" language. For example, "I felt hurt and sad."

3) "WHY did you pick that restaurant?": "Why" questions often come across as critical, even though that is not how we might intend them. Instead, consider asking "what" questions, such as "What do you like about this restaurant?"

4) "BUT": Starting a sentence with a connection phrase, such as "I really love you" and then using the word "but" can negate the meaning behind the initial connection phrase. Consider using "and" instead. For example, "I really love you *and* I would like to work on our communication styles."

5) "What were you thinking?": Criticism often exacerbates conflicts and is less likely to get our needs met. Instead, strategies for working

together on resolving the conflict can be helpful. For example, "Let's think of ways to reduce these conflicts in the future."

6) "Everyone else does it this way" or "My friend/therapist thinks you're wrong": Bringing other people's lifestyles or opinions into an argument can make the other person feel as if they are ganged up against and can make them defensive. Instead, consider making it specific to you and the person you're speaking with. For example, "How would you feel if we tried a different strategy?"

Connection communication:

Connection communication is both vulnerable and assertive. It allows you to communicate your feelings and your needs with someone else, and to work together as a team to reduce conflicts. In situations in which you're upset, it may be helpful to take some time to reflect on what you are feeling (at the tip of the iceberg) and what you actually need (at the core of the iceberg). When reflecting on this, it may be helpful to focus on what you want to get out of your communication and then have a discussion with the intended person.

Connection-style communication might look like this:

- Noticing and reflecting about the specific situation and your emotions before reacting.
  For example, your friend might have canceled on you several times, and you might be feeling frustrated, rejected, and hurt.
- Figuring out what your needs are.
  For example, for your friend to be more reliable.
- Expressing respect, how much this person means to you.
  For example, "You are one of my closest friends..."
- AND
  Using "and" instead of "but" in assertive conversations can increase connection and reduce defensiveness.

- In this specific situation...
  For example, "Last week when you canceled our plans..."
- *I feel...*
  Using "I" language instead of "you" language. For example, "I felt sad and disappointed."
- It would mean a lot to me if we worked on...
  For example, "It would mean a lot to me if we worked on letting each other know as soon as possible if we can't hang out."
- Expressing gratitude.
  For example, "Thank you for talking to me about this."
- Reinforcing the behavior.
  Acknowledging when the person does what you asked them to. For example, "Thank you for telling me ahead of time, I really appreciate that."

Seeing these patterns of communication, what do you notice?

"I see a lot of disconnection pattern between me and my husband," Hannah says. "I think that I'm passive and he's aggressive. And at times, we can both be aggressive."

"Thank you so much for sharing that, Hannah," I say. "Would you be willing to tell us a little more about it?"

"Sure. He criticizes me for not being able to pick up our daughter. He shames me and calls me a 'bad mother.' I shut down and walk away. Sometimes, I get so tired of his insults that I lash out and then we both yell at each other."

"It must be excruciating to be shamed for something that is already so challenging for you."

She nods. "It's awful. I think he thinks that I don't want to parent her. But I do. More than anything."

"What might you need in those moments when you want to be closer to your daughter and you may be feeling scared to do so?"

"I guess...just for him to understand how hard this is for me. Maybe to hold my hand or to gently encourage me to try holding her without yelling at me."

"That's fair. How might you ask him to provide that for you?"

She thinks about it for a moment. "Maybe something along the lines of: *I love you. You and Sarah mean everything to me. I understand your frustration and I really want to work on being able to hold our daughter and take care of her. When you call me a bad mom, I feel ashamed and deeply hurt. This statement reinforces what I already think about myself. It would mean so much to me if we could work on this together, if maybe you could hold my hand and encourage me to hold her, then I think I will over time find the courage to do it. Thank you for taking care of her and thank you for hearing me out.*"

I smile at her. "That was a wonderful example of connection communication. How did that feel?"

"Good," she says. "I'm feeling really anxious about it, but I want to try it."

When we are shamed, yelled at, or rejected by a parent, friend, or a romantic partner, we might shut down, feeling shame not only emotionally, but also physically—for example, in our lower body, sometimes as a paralyzing feeling, making us unable to move. However, when a trusted partner or friend says something gentle or supportive, it can change everything.[39] It can give us the courage we didn't know we had and can *encourage* us to take active steps to connect with our loved ones, our core values, and ourselves.

Zaara raises her hand. "I told my boyfriend that something bad happened to me, but I couldn't bring myself to tell him the full story yet."

"That was a very courageous choice, Zaara," I tell her. "How did it go?"

"I cried. He didn't push. He...he just held me and said that he will never make me do anything that makes me feel uncomfortable."

"That sounds so nice," Tala says. "My boyfriend doesn't hold me when I cry. He tells me that I'm being 'dramatic.' And if I try to argue, he yells at me, and if I yell back, then he threatens to leave me, or walks away from me, or hangs up on me if we are on the phone. It makes me so infuriated when he does that, that I sometimes scream at him not to leave or beg him to stay. I'm not myself when he does that. He calls me 'crazy' when I'm like that. I don't know why we seem to bring out the worst in each other, but I'm not me when we fight."

My dad was my mom's drug dealer, and that's how I came to be. When I was seventeen, the abuse got severe enough I nearly died by my mother's hand.

At the height of my trauma, I was numb. In the moment I saw this as some sort of strength, but looking back I realize it was a protection against feeling all the pain I felt. But as time went by that pain slipped in. I started having flashbacks and remembering things I had blocked out. I began to notice that some triggers would lead to a full "shutdown." My mind would go fuzzy and I would just freeze. This impaired my driving and made relationships difficult as I could not communicate my feelings.

I made the simple choice to survive. It seems small or even a no-brainer, but at the moment the pull to give up was too strong. Deciding to survive was the first step in overcoming. The next, and probably the most significant point, came a few years later as I left my abusive family. My husband and I faced a new challenge as we discovered we were not able to have children. It was another blow that had the ability to make or break me. Then my husband said the life-changing words: "What's your new dream?" I had hardly been given the chance to dream, and this phrase opened a floodgate of desires I never knew I had.

A few months later I enrolled in my first college class at the age of twenty-two. The final metamorphosis would come after completing my MS. The day I decided to apply for a doctorate of psychology program I did it for me, and me alone.

If you need help, please see a counselor. These are people who are trained and want to help, so let them. There is absolutely no shame in being a victim of abuse. You are a survivor and stronger than you know. This story is an inspiration for not only others but should be an inspiration to yourself.

Finally, take care of yourself. Abuse can make you feel small and insignificant and can reinforce ideas of pleasing others in order to protect yourself. Learn to make yourself a priority. You are safe now to live the quality of life you deserve.

—Hannah

"That sounds heartbreaking, Tala," I tell her. "One of the cruelest, most heartbreaking experiences we can go through is punishment by rejection. To be in solitary confinement with our thoughts and feelings, and our broken heart, can feel like we're dying, and we will do anything to make it stop."

"Yes," she says. "Exactly. I feel like he's punishing me by being rejecting. And when he does that, I feel like I'm suffocating. I keep on trying to fight for us, and it feels like I'm fighting for my life. It feels like I'm screaming for him to hear me, but the louder I yell, the less he hears me. It hurts so badly." She looks down, her voice breaking at the end of her sentence.

No matter how much we disagree with others, we always deserve to be treated with respect. Even in a fight, we can still be kind and affectionate, and we deserve to be treated in a kind and affectionate way.

Sometimes, when emotions run high, it can be helpful to take a short break, to breathe, and figure out what we would like to communicate to the person with whom we might be having a disagreement. It is perfectly okay to take space to do this, and it is *crucial* to communicate that *you will return* and *when* you will return so as not to make it seem as though you are leaving this person forever. For example, it might be helpful to say, "I'm going to step out for ten minutes to cool off and then I will return, and we can work this out."

Similarly, a rejection of a physical comfort, such as a hug, during a fight can feel extremely painful. In fact, maintaining physical contact, such as hand-holding and eye contact, can often de-escalate the fight because such physical contact can allow for physical and emotional support while the conflict is happening. Furthermore, when we are emotionally and physically connecting with a loved one, such as through a hug or hand-holding, our bodies release *oxytocin* (also known as the "cuddle hormone"), which can soothe some of our physical and emotional distress. This means that by maintaining support for one another during a conflict with a loved one, we are likely to reduce the intensity of these conflicts (the exceptions to that are if there is a danger to someone's safety or a presence of physical violence).

One of the most damaging things we can do or experience is the withdrawal of affection because of a conflict. What this may inadvertently convey is "Because of this conflict, you do not deserve to be loved. You are unlovable." Unless there is a presence of abuse, violence, or infidelity, for example, rejection in this way may be an extremely harsh punishment. If you reject your loved one this way, think about whether this is actually the message you're trying to convey. If you are being rejected this way by your loved one, it may be important to explain this to them at a calm time and create other safety parameters, so that during conflict you can still support each other. Remember that you can be angry with someone and still love them at the same time.

The goal is not necessarily to fight less; rather, it is to have adaptive disagreements and discourse, which can allow you to understand each other, and to find support and safety, bringing you closer together. Such adaptive disagreements can essentially become helpful *learning experiences*, creating a stronger emotional bond with that person.

Sometimes, no matter how kind and open we may be with others, no matter how many attempts we may try to make to create meaningful connection with family members, friends, or romantic partners, we may still feel unheard, invalidated, and misunderstood. This does not mean that we are doing something wrong. It may mean that we have different forms of connection and different needs than other people in our life. Our needs for connection are valid and allowed, and if the people in your life struggle to meet them, then we may look to other forms of creating meaningful connection for the specific kind of support that we are looking for, such as joining support groups and communities with similar interests. Another way of connecting with our loved ones is through learning about love languages.

Love languages

Most people may not realize that everyone—not only romantic partners but all people, friends, family members, anyone who loves someone else—may have a different way of expressing their love language. A love language is a way of expressing appreciation, support, and gratitude for our loved ones. One of the most groundbreaking works to help us understand how people in relationships communicate is *The 5 Love Languages,* by marriage and family counselor Gary Chapman. Chapman breaks down our connection needs into five language categories: *words of affirmation* (such as verbal expression of gratitude), *acts of service* (such as bringing someone a hot cup of tea), *gifts* (such as small tokens of appreciation), *quality time* (spending time together in a meaningful way), and *physical touch* (such as a hug or holding one's hand).[40]

Although traditionally these love languages primarily applied to romantic partners, they can also apply to all intimate and close relationships, such as friendships, relationships with family members, and others. We might even have a different love language with different loved ones in our lives. For example, we might have a preference for receiving physical affection from our romantic partner or our pet, while instead wanting to receive words of affirmation from our friends or parents. By understanding our specific needs for connection with the important people in our life, we may be able to ask for what we need and provide our loved ones with what they need as well.

Superhero Training Step: What might be some ways in which you have received connection from your loved ones, and what might be some ways in which you would like to receive support from your loved ones?

You deserve to be treated with kindness and respect. What might be a way to ask for what you *do* want as opposed to asking for what you *don't* want?

If your loved ones are unable to give you what you need, is there someone who can support you in a difficult moment? Perhaps a friend, a fandom, a support group, a pet, an online community, or a fictional character?

Take as much time as you need with this reflection practice. There is no obligation to complete it. If you decide that you would like to try it, and if at any point you need to take a breath or a break, please give yourself the permission to do so.

Chapter 6

The Mind's Dungeons and the Emotion Dragons

Growing up in Ukraine meant that the Chinese zodiac, or *sheng xiao*, was a strong part of our culture. The Chinese zodiac spans a twelve-year cycle, each year representing a different animal. In both the Chinese and Ukrainian cultures, people born as a particular zodiac sign are believed to inherit those characteristics.

I was born in the year of the pig. So was my father.

According to the Chinese zodiac, people born in the year of the pig are lazy, clumsy, messy, can be prone to addiction and gluttony, and can be overweight.

"You're a pig, just like your father."

This phrase was razor-etched into my mind. When I would forget to make my bed, forget to hang up my shirt and instead fold it over the back of my chair, or when I would get a stain on my dress, my mother would call me a pig, proclaiming both my father and me to be pigs together.

On the surface, it seemed like teasing. And then I started to notice a pattern. When my father would come home late, when he would lie around rather than help her with the house chores, when he would vomit yet again from another bender, when he would throw garbage onto the same plates that had his food, she would call him a pig. And me.

When I would ask her to stop saying it, her response was, "I am just stating the facts. You were born in the year of the pig. Just like your father."

I hated everything related to the term. I hated pink. I hated pigs and children's stories of pigs. I hated everything that ever earned me the title of a pig—from unmade beds, to clothes that weren't put away, to even the smell of alcohol.

Having spent years trying to prove to my mother and to myself that I was indeed not a pig, I was mortified at being seen as messy, lazy, or gluttonous, especially around my mother.

When I gained weight in my mid-twenties, I heard that word ringing through my own ears whenever I would look into the mirror. I was so desperate to prove that I was not "a pig" that I would have anxiety attacks over having a guest when my house was not perfectly neat, as well as about my weight. I tried dozens of diets and started numerous workout programs, all because I was trying to outrun my own mental dungeon. When I had guests, I would spend days cleaning to prepare and spend most of their visits cleaning as well. I was so attached to the idea of not being a pig that I forgot that I was a person. Somewhere in the midst of my trying to run away from my pain, I ran away from myself. I spent my days focusing on running away from emotions I did not want to feel, such as deep, devastating shame, self-disgust, as well as depression and anger. I binged on television shows and kept myself extremely busy with academics. I earned multiple graduate degrees and worked four or five part-time jobs at a time. Somehow, in my mind, I was trying to justify to myself that if I am working myself this hard, then I cannot possibly be lazy. And if I am not lazy, then I cannot possibly be a pig.

We often tell ourselves that we cannot do certain things, such as go to an amusement park, ask someone out on a date, or eat in public, until we are thin, less anxious, in less pain, and so on. Our mind dungeon might attack us like school bullies, telling us that we are not allowed to enjoy our experiences, including dating, eating, resting, having sex, or having a day off. We believe that we have to delay doing something for ourselves until we have proven to the world that we are worthy of it.

"That's how I have felt my entire life," Lisa says. "My mom got me into a fat camp when I was eight years old. My very thin sister got toast with jam for breakfast every morning. I got a small plate of fruit. At twelve, my mom started me on diet pills, which made me feel sick. But it didn't even matter.

"When I was thirteen, I started sneaking food into my bedroom and hiding it. The day my mother found out was the day I seriously considered suicide. I tried explaining to her that I was not eating enough and that I was always hungry, which was extremely difficult to do. Fighting for my right to eat and insisting that I was not eating enough was already extremely triggering for me.

"My mom brought me out into the living room and pointed to my sister. She said, 'Look at your sister and look at you. Which one of you is not eating enough?' I remember feeling incredibly ashamed of my body, comparing it to my sister's, as I've always done, but somehow feeling worse at the intentionality in which this was done.

"I began starving myself on purpose. I went four months mostly drinking two gallons of water a day, learning to ignore my own hunger, and eating a small handful of nuts during the day. I lost twenty pounds. I also lost my period, I lost the color in my face, and started losing some of my hair.

"It was the only time in my life my mother told me she was proud of me.

"When I fainted in school, I was taken to the emergency room. The doctor told my mom that I was dangerously malnourished and that I had to go to an inpatient eating disorders clinic for immediate treatment.

"My mother tried to argue that I could not possibly be malnourished. That was when the doctor explained to her that our weight and our health are not the same. That people could be fat and be completely healthy, and that someone could be fat and anorexic at the same time. She explained to my mom that people could be thin and at the same time could be at a high risk for heart disease. She explained that it's the type of food we eat and the amount of exercise we partake in that really make a difference in the person's health, not their weight or BMI. And she also said that if I didn't start eating more, I could die.

"I was terrified to start eating again. The eating disorders program was extremely difficult, but it saved my life. The doctors and other providers there were very nice and supportive, and saw me as a person instead of only seeing me for my weight. I made new friends in the program and some of them are still my good friends.

"I am now eating no differently from my other healthy friends, but I find that, to this day, the messages I implicitly or explicitly received from my mother still haunt me. I judge myself for eating a burger, even though I only have it once a year. Believe me. I count.

"Strangers still congratulate me when they see me eating a salad or working out in a gym. They may mean it to be supportive, but I feel singled out because they do not treat thin people the same way they treat me. I still shy away from going to some social events because I am afraid of other people judging me. There are still places I have not traveled to, because my mind is telling me that I cannot go there until I lose weight. I've been waiting to live my entire life. I've been wanting to travel to Paris, but I'm terrified of going and being fat-shamed there. I have been procrastinating *me*, waiting until I reach some kind of an unrealistic, society-mandated, thin ideal.

"And I am starting to realize that I've been kept prisoner to this ideal for way too long. I am ready to set myself free of this sizeist culture and I am ready to start living. I want to learn to accept my body and myself. I want to learn to love my curves, my rolls, and my stomach instead of being disgusted by them. I want to buy a sexy swimsuit and go to the beach. I haven't been to the beach since I was a small child. I want to feel like I have the same universal rights as my thin friends and be treated as a human—with acceptance and respect."

"Wow," Victoria says. "That was deep. I really appreciate you sharing that. I'm sorry about the way your mom treated you. That's not right and I can see how it's still with you to this day. I can relate to that and I wish I had your courage to accept myself. It's still hard for me, with the messages I've gotten and still get... I don't know how not to allow them to trap me."

"Lisa, Victoria," I say. "Thank you both for sharing. Your stories resonate with countless women worldwide, who've also experienced rejection, prejudice, sizeism, fat phobia, transphobia, and misogyny. And your stories can help others who are going through similar experiences."

Victoria puts her head down. "I don't think I can help anyone."

"What makes you say that?" I ask her.

She shakes her head. "I haven't beaten it. It's with me every day. I spend all day wondering if I am feminine enough, if I'm passing enough. My bones are bigger than other women I know, so I feel bigger. I also starved myself in the past and still deny myself desserts and comfort foods. But more than that, I don't allow myself to be seen. I have this thought that keeps telling me that if I don't look enough like a woman, then I don't deserve to be treated as one.

"That's why it hurts so much when someone misgenders me. It's like they're confirming what I already fear. The other day I went into the ladies' room and a woman in there told me that I don't belong there. I looked at her and said, 'Lady, I don't belong anywhere.' I constantly feel like I'm in between worlds, you know? Not quite a part of this world or that one. I'm scared to date. Terrified. Because I think it would break me if someone rejected me.

"I hear transphobic slurs and I'm tired of people asking me if I'm in the right place because most of the time I don't think there is a right place for me. I just want to belong. I just want to be seen. But the idea of it scares the shit out of me."

"Victoria, thank you so much for sharing your experiences. I am so sorry about the way you have been treated. No one deserves that and everyone deserves to be treated with respect.

"You said something very powerful a minute ago. You said that you don't think you can help anyone because you haven't 'beaten it.' I think oftentimes there is an assumption that a battle with some kind of a difficulty is a win-or-lose kind of a game. The truth is that all of these battles are ongoing. Winning does not mean that we have no symptoms. All we need to do is to be there. In the battle. Sometimes the battle may end one way and sometimes another. But being in the battle in the first place—that is winning. To be present when it gets rough. To face obstacles that we do every day. Each and every one of you is already a winner. A warrior. Each one of you is a Super-Woman."

Is there anything you would like to share with the group, either to support the group members who've already spoken or to share your own story? Think of your journal as a safe space where you can choose to share, not share, or share as much or as little as you'd like.

"Thank you so much for that, it means a lot to me and it makes it easier for me to share," Isabella says. "People often tell me to be strong. To fight my cancer. Not to allow it to win. And there are times when I feel like I am losing—days when I can't get out of bed. There are days where I don't know if I will survive another treatment. The cancer may be in remission, but I am still in treatment and I don't know if or when it will end. And there are some days when I don't want to do it anymore. I always felt weak when I felt that way."

"And now?" I ask her.

"Now I am starting to see how our thoughts and feelings might sometimes imprison us in our own torture chamber. I guess because we know what we are most afraid of, our mind might know exactly how to inflict the most pain. So, how do we get rid of these thoughts and feelings?"

The avoidance paradox

When it comes to our trying to resist or escape our cognitive (thoughts) and emotional experiences, avoidance behaviors tend to backfire. The more we try to stay within our safety zone, such as our room, our house, or any other location or situation in which we attempt to hide from our uncomfortable thoughts and emotions, the more anxious/depressed we might actually feel. That is because the very thoughts and emotions we are trying to run away from *live* in the safety zone. Therefore, an attempt to run away from our painful emotions is almost like moving in with them, locking the door and throwing away the key. So, the more we try to avoid difficult emotions or painful thoughts, the more suffocating these experiences can be because we are literally rooming with them.

Most people report that in the short term, if they are able to stay inside their safety zone (for example, avoiding going to a social event when they are feeling too anxious to go), they might feel relieved. And sometimes, when we have been exhausted by our emotional struggles, taking a little break can actually be helpful, in that it can restore our energy, allowing us the endurance we need to get back into the battle. However, hiding out in the safety zone for too long a time can lead to us overrelying on running away from discomfort and losing the ability to trust ourselves to handle difficult experiences. I am, of course, not referring to situations in which our physical safety might be compromised—only our perceived cognitive and emotional experiences. The more we try to get rid of difficult thoughts, emotions, and internal sensations, the more we might be reinforcing the belief that we are not capable of facing our internal dragons. This means that the longer we stay in our safety zone, the *more* of those painful thoughts and emotions we are likely to feel.

Instead of getting rid of these painful thoughts and experiences, instead of hiding away from them, the opposite way of managing them is through stepping out of our comfort zone into the *connection zone*. This will not be easy, and it may mean that initially the difficult emotions and the scary thoughts become louder. Actually, we tend to feel worse in the *anticipation* of leaving our safety zone. However, most people find that once they step out of their safety zone, their experiences are not as overwhelming as they initially anticipated.

Does this mean that stepping outside of your safety zone will get rid of your unwanted thoughts and emotions? Of course not.

But what it does mean is that challenging yourself to make a connection with people and activities you care about is more important than focusing on running away from uncomfortable thoughts and feelings. It's not about running away from what you don't want—it's about taking active steps to connect with what you *do* want regardless of the uncomfortable thoughts and feelings, because that type of connection may be worth the discomfort.

I sometimes like to think of it as a bull's-eye model in which staying in the safety zone is the center of the bull's-eye. Stepping outside of our comfort zone in order to find and create meaningful connection is the next circle of the bull's-eye. This step may be challenging, and it can also be worth it if it means finding a meaningful connection to your passions, your loved ones, or your sense of purpose. On the outside of the connection zone is the "overwhelm zone," which refers to forcing yourself to suffer. Staying in this zone may be toxic, damaging, or too triggering and overwhelming to be helpful. There is no need to push yourself so hard that you will end up suffering. Emotional safety and meaningful connection are both necessary to create a sense of balance for ourselves.

"Has anyone ever experienced something like this?" I ask. "Have any of you ever tried to run away from your painful experiences and found that it became more and more challenging to face them outside of your safety zone over time?"

"I think this is what happened to me," Divya says. "I am always really vigilant about my pain. To be fair, I am in pain all the time. But I guess, looking at this model, I think that what I've been doing is staying at home so much that I'm not engaging in things that are meaningful to me because I'm afraid of making my pain worse."

"Thank you for sharing that, Divya," I say. "It makes sense. We, as human beings, naturally want to escape painful and uncomfortable experiences, and may naturally wish to avoid situations that might exacerbate our pain or discomfort. And I imagine that, to some degree, it was helpful to do so, as avoiding some of those activities might have prevented you from worsening your physical pain. What has been the cost of that?"

Divya thinks about it. "I guess... not spending time with my family. I missed my daughter's school play because I didn't want to be in pain watching it. I missed my friend's wedding. And last year, my husband wanted to take the kids to an amusement park. I knew that walking around all day would be too much for me, so I didn't go with them. I guess that when it comes to my pain, I'm so scared of being in the overwhelm zone, that I don't even try to leave my safety zone. I didn't realize that there was a middle option."

"That's me as well," Hannah says. "Looking at this model, I'm definitely spending so much of my time in the safety zone, to try to avoid my anxiety, that I haven't actually realized until just now that my anxiety hasn't gotten better in remaining in the safety zone. It got progressively worse. I don't trust myself with the things that I used to, and I don't feel connected to myself, my daughter, or my husband. It's interesting, I always thought that stepping outside of my safety zone would mean that I am stepping directly into overwhelm, but like Divya I also didn't realize that there was a gentler option."

To outsiders I don't have much of an origin story. I never wanted for any necessity, my parents love each other, and I was always encouraged to pursue the things I found interesting.

On the inside, I was constantly fighting to keep my head above water. I have ADHD, sensory processing disorder, depression, anxiety, and panic attacks that were all undiagnosed until my early to mid-twenties. Some of my worst symptoms are emotional dysregulation, inability to function in a crowded environment, constant daydreaming, and an inability to focus on tasks that I find boring.

One of my key turning points happened when I first started working with an ADHD coach. She looked me in the eye and said, "Not everything is about you, you didn't break the world so you can't fix the world."

If you are on a similar journey of self-love, remember that *you are worth loving*! Remember that you didn't break the world and you can't fix the entire world.

—Maggie

The mind dungeons and emotion dragons

Previously, we learned to identify our cognitive factors (our thoughts) and how they can affect how we might feel and act. Our mind is like a highly functioning computer that performs numerous tasks, such as planning, analyzing, remembering, reflecting, and creating, often at the same time. One of its main tasks is threat assessment.[41]

That means that unless we are specifically focused on a given task (i.e., are mindful about what we are doing), our mind's function will be to keep us safe from potential danger. Like an overprotective parent or bodyguard, our mind often assumes that the probability of danger is higher than it actually might be. In many ways, the ongoing threat assessment can be very helpful. For example, our threat assessment system might warn us, "If you do not prepare your presentation, you could lose your job." In this case, this thought and the feelings of anxiety that accompany it are actually helpful in that they might encourage us to prepare for our presentation.

In fact, psychologist and researcher Dr. Kelly McGonigal states that stress (and anxiety) may actually be beneficial for us. It seems that stress orients us to our core values, waking up our adrenaline system to help us function in order to meet our goals. Our pounding heart may actually be helping us to circulate the blood around the body, allowing us to think faster, respond quicker, and be better prepared for the task we are required to do.[42]

Interestingly, our experiences of physical or emotional distress (our *raw pain*) can oftentimes be exacerbated by our unwillingness to experience it (our *muddled pain*).[43] Raw pain is the direct experience that we have, such as a painful headache or the feeling of anxiety. Muddled pain is raw pain *plus* the resistance of that pain (for example, having a thought, *Why do I always have to feel anxious? I never get a break!*).

Have any of you ever felt this way?

"Huh," Divya reflects. "Yes, I have. There are days when my raw physical pain is a six out of ten, but when I start thinking about how this pain will never go away, my muddled pain can be a ten out of ten."

Observing our raw experiences can make them more tolerable over time. Our willingness to experience our raw pain can increase when we remember what is truly important to us, even if the raw pain doesn't actually get better. Here are some guiding questions we can use to practice strengthening these skills:

1. What is the situation? What's happening? How am I interpreting this situation?
2. On a scale of 0–10, what is my raw pain right now?
3. On a scale of 0–10, what is my muddled pain right now?
4. What is the evidence to support my interpretation of the situation?
5. What is the evidence against this thought?
6. What's happened in the past and how did I handle it?
7. What do I want? (Think from the core of the iceberg, such as correction, love, and acceptance.)

8. How important is this to me?
9. How can I build emotional and physical safety for myself in this situation to help me accomplish my goal?
10. Would it be worth the discomfort of going outside of the comfort zone if it means doing something really meaningful to me?

"Would anyone like to try these?" I ask.

"I can try it," Tala says. "Okay. Yesterday, my boyfriend went to hang out with his friends and his ex-girlfriend was there as well."

"Great example, Tala. That was the situation. What were your raw and muddled emotions then?"

"I guess my raw emotions were insecurity and jealousy and my raw thoughts were, *I'm not comfortable with him hanging out with her.* And my muddled thoughts were, *He's going to cheat on me* and *I am stupid for jumping to conclusions and for being jealous.* I felt ashamed for feeling jealous and angry at him and at myself when I thought that he might cheat on me."

"Thank you so much for sharing that, Tala. You identified a few very human and universal emotions—insecurity and jealousy. We feel these emotions when we are afraid of losing someone or something very important to us, and given your history, it makes sense that you might feel that way in this situation. When you focused on just your raw emotions, what was your raw pain?"

"Just the emotions of insecurity and jealousy? About a six out of ten."

"How about your muddled pain? This would be your raw pain plus the self-shame about your feeling this way."

"That was much worse. Probably a ten out of ten."

"Great job on noticing that, Tala," I say. "Who would like to try the next two questions?"

Hannah raises her hand. "I would. Okay. My thought tends to be that if I pick up my daughter, that I will end up harming her. I guess there's no actual evidence for that thought other than my anxiety telling me that I would. As far as evidence against this thought, I have held her in the past, I've never physically hurt anyone in my life, and I love her very much and I want to protect her. There was one time two weeks ago, when my husband was out of town, and I was alone with my daughter. I was very anxious, but I was able to take care of her. I guess... if I did it once, then I can try it again."

"Great job, Hannah. I love how you were able to use your past experiences to help yourself. Who would like to try the remaining questions?"

Zaara volunteers. "I can try it. Ever since the assault, I've shut down and disconnected from almost everyone. I would like to tell my best friend, but I am scared that she will judge me or tell my community about it, which could lead to me and my family being shamed or kicked out of the community. So, I suppose, to answer questions six and seven, what I want is to be close to my friend again and to be honest with her. It is *very* important to me. As far as the last two questions, I can try letting her know slowly over time. Perhaps I could tell her on a day when I would be able to come here afterward to receive support, if I need it. That might help me to build some emotional safety. Regarding the last question, this is very challenging because I am terrified of losing my friend, but I also realize that because I haven't talked to her about this, we haven't been close at all. I think it may be worth the discomfort of my fear to tell her if it means that we have a chance of being close again."

"What a courageous choice, Zaara!" I say. "I am proud of you for planning to take this step outside of your comfort zone to connect with your best friend in this way. And I love that you are considering setting up emotional support for yourself in planning to tell her on a day when you would be able to come here, to the sanctuary, and to receive group support after you tell her."

Zaara provided a powerful example of an action she would like to take to step outside of her comfort zone: telling her friend about her assault. Here are some other examples of stepping outside of our comfort zone:

- Reaching out to a friend
- Going out for a cup of tea or coffee
- Committing five minutes to work on a project you have been procrastinating on
- Telling a friend you miss them
- Asking a loved one for a hug

Before we begin to take steps outside of our comfort zone, our emotions might actually rile up. Our emotions are kind of like dragons. They can be strong and intimidating, but they are also magical. We can take a step back and observe them in all their beauty, seeing them soar. After a while, we may be able to notice that they can be enormous sometimes, but they are not dangerous.

Just as our emotions are not dangerous, our thoughts are not dangerous either. Sometimes, our society- or self-imposed labels and narratives can affect how we feel about ourselves. For example, people who are bullied about their appearance may begin to believe the label that they were assigned by their bully. Similarly, we might sometimes shame our own selves, bullying ourselves, and might self-prescribe certain painful labels to ourselves. This is a habitual narrative, meaning that we have believed it for so long that it has become a habit.

Here are the most common habitual narratives that some people might have:

- I am a loser
- I am a failure
- I am not good enough
- I am not attractive enough
- I am weird, awkward, or strange
- I have to change the way I look or feel before I can be happy
- It's my fault that the assault happened
- It's my fault that I feel this way

Our labels and experiences do not define us. What ultimately defines us are our actions, our core values—what we do and what we stand for. This is the superhero narrative. In adjusting our narrative from our habitual narrative to a superhero narrative, we can focus on our strengths and we become able to see our whole self more objectively.

Let's work on introducing yourself to the group using your superhero narrative.

Lisa volunteers to go first. "I have been judged by my weight, but my weight does not define me. I'm a lawyer, a sister, a daughter, and friend. I am a coffee connoisseur and someone who fights for equality both in my work and in my personal life. I am a woman. A Super-Woman. My drive is my superpower and that is what defines me."

Victoria high-fives her. "I have experienced racism, transphobia, and prejudice, and that does not define me. I am a human being. I am a veterinary assistant, a cat lover, a loyal friend, and someone who loves to travel. I am someone who's been hurt and who wants to be loved and accepted. I am a woman. I am a black woman. A Super-Woman and that is what defines me."

"I'm someone who experienced sexual assault and that does not define me," Zaara says. "I am a pre-med student, I am a Super-Woman, I care about helping people. My compassion is my superpower and that is what defines me."

"I survived cancer and that does not define me," Isabella says. "I have been rejected by my parents over my sexual orientation, but my parents do not define me. I am not organized or punctual and that is a part of me, too. I am a hairdresser, an artist, a poet, and someone who is a damn good cook. I am a superhero because I often do the impossible. And that is what defines me."

"My disability does not define me," Divya says. "I am a wife and a mother. A full-time student. I am a friend and a daughter. I battle my dragons on a daily basis. I am a Super-Woman and my persistence is my superpower and that is what defines me."

"I am someone who experienced years of emotional abuse and invalidation and that does not define me," Tala says. "I am a Super-Woman. I try to help my friends and other people, even if I don't know them. Helping people is my superpower and that is what defines me."

If you are willing, please pull out your journal again and take a moment to introduce yourself to the group using your superhero narrative.

"Nice!" Hannah says, smiling. "For me, my anxiety does not define me. I am a mother, a wife, a daughter, and a friend. I battle my own dragons every day. I am a Super-Woman and that is what defines me."

So, to summarize:

- You are not what happened to you
- You are not what people call you
- You are not your weight
- You are not what your parents demand you to be
- You are not your anxiety
- You are not the mistakes you make
- You are not your mental health struggle

You are:

- A person that battles dragons on a daily basis
- Your actions
- Your core values
- Loved
- Allowed to be you
- Allowed to take care of your own needs too
- Allowed to be happy
- Allowed to feel safe and respected
- Allowed to rest
- Allowed to have a bad day
- Allowed to make mistakes
- A Super-Woman

Superhero Training Step: If you are willing, take some time to notice some of your own mind dungeons and emotion dragons. See if you can step back and just observe them. See whether they might be helpful. See if you can write down some small steps you would be willing to commit to taking outside of your safety zone and into your connection zone. These do not have to be big steps; give yourself the support and safety that you need to try it. Feel free to use the #SuperWomen hashtag on social media to find other super-women around the world. Remember, anticipatory anxiety (anxiety before you step out of the comfort zone) is nearly always worse than when you actually step out into the connection zone. See if you can write down some of the steps you would be willing to practice this week and track how it went.

Take as much time as you need. You are not alone. You have already battled thousands of dragons in your lifetime. You are already a warrior. You are a superhero. I believe in you.

Chapter 7

The Shield of Self-Compassion

I looked at the clock. Thirteen hours left in my workday. I am used to working long hours and I love my job. But that day, I felt as if I had just gotten off a rocky boat. I was extremely light-headed, and my vision was starting to blur. I told myself that I would just go to sleep as soon as I got home.

Twelve hours left.

My heart started pounding louder, as my vision became worse. *Get yourself together*, I said to myself.

Eight hours left.

I felt both hungry and nauseated at the same time. Forcing myself to have a protein shake in between seeing my clients and chugging some water, I felt a little clearer.

Six hours left.

Usually, my days fly by, seeing client after client, which is both rewarding and exciting for me. I love being able to help others, and I love being a source of support for other people. It gives me a sense of purpose. This day, I found myself longing to be home, in bed, next to my husband and my two cats. *Don't be weak*, I told myself. *You have work to do.*

Four hours left.

My mouth felt dry, despite me drinking more water than usual. My hands felt clammy and I could barely stand up to let my clients in and out of the office.

Three hours left.

Something felt very wrong. I nearly fell over when greeting my client, and I had trouble understanding what she was saying to me. I texted my husband in between sessions and he insisted that I cancel the rest of my clients and let him take me to the emergency room. I refused, thinking, *I'm just making a big deal over nothing.*

Two hours left.

I canceled my last session, a group, but decided to see one more client, who was already in the waiting room. I could barely see her because my vision was almost completely gone.

When I got out of work, my husband wanted to take me to the emergency room, while I wanted to go home. We compromised on going to a walk-in clinic. By the time I got up to the front desk, I was slurring words and had to be propped up to stand. The intake coordinator insisted that I needed to be seen right away, ahead of the people waiting there, and within minutes, the nurse took my vitals. She ran to get the physician's assistant, who told me to go to the emergency room immediately.

Thankfully, it wasn't a stroke. It wasn't a seizure. It wasn't a heart attack. But it was an emergency. It was burnout. My blood pressure was dangerously high, and my body was severely starved of rest, so it was failing to perform basic functions, such as standing, walking, seeing, and information processing.

Although I understood that burnout can lead to physical fatigue and mental exhaustion, I never realized that it could actually be physiologically dangerous. In addition to the physical and mental exhaustion, prolonged burnout can lead to a stroke, heart attack, or sudden cardiac death.[44]

I was ordered to take several days off from work and to focus on self-care. It took three days for some of my symptoms to remit, and over two weeks for me to feel "back to normal." A few days after my hospital visit, I found out that not one, but two of my female friends, both under the age of thirty-five, were previously hospitalized for strokes due to burnout.

So, what is burnout exactly?

In May 2019, the World Health Organization (WHO) released a statement that burnout is to be recognized as an occupational phenomenon to be included in the International Classification of Diseases (ICD-11). Burnout typically occurs when someone is exposed to a stressful work environment for an extended period of time. However, burnout can also occur in situations in which someone experiences prolonged emotional distress due to their environment (for example, acting as a caregiver for a loved one), as well as when someone works an extensive amount of time, even if they enjoy their job, as I enjoy mine. Burnout symptoms include fatigue; sleep problems; mental fog; dizziness and balance issues; not wanting to be around one's coworkers, clients, or loved ones; difficulty getting out of bed; job dissatisfaction; frequent illness (cold, flu, and other illnesses), inflammatory illnesses and flare-ups; changes in weight or appetite; irritability; depression; and/or suicidal thoughts.[45] [46] In addition, burnout accounts for more than 80 percent of work-related mistakes, meaning that most work-related mistakes occur because of burnout, and the more burned out we are, the more likely we are to make a mistake at work.[47] What it also means is that if we make a mistake, it could be an indication that we need rest and support, as opposed to an indication that we need to blame or shame ourselves.

Burnout is a worldwide phenomenon, although in some countries it is more prevalent than others. In Japan, the occurrence of burnout-related deaths has gotten so high, that there is a special name for this phenomenon: *karōshi* (過労死).[48] Researchers approximate that 40 percent of Japanese physicians die by *karōshi.*[49] According to statistical reports, approximately 330 confirmed cases of brain- and heart-related deaths occurred because of *karōshi* in Japan between 2002 and 2005, although the total number of claimed *karōshi* cases was actually 869. In addition, the likelihood of *karōshi* appears to be related to the number of hours one works, meaning that the more hours one might work, the higher the potential risk of dying prematurely.[50] Although the term *karōshi* includes death or permanent disability due to a burnout-related event, such as a heart attack or a stroke, it does not include incidents in which the worker dies due to an accident caused by burnout, meaning that the number of deaths related to burnout could be significantly higher than actually reported.[51] A study conducted in Finland followed more than seven thousand workers for ten years, measuring their burnout rates and studying their health. The results of the study found that workers under the age of forty-five who scored just one unit higher on the burnout measure were 35 percent more likely to die during that ten-year period compared to workers who scored one unit lower on the burnout measure.[52]

One way to think about this is to consider how we treat our devices—primarily our phones. When our phones run low on battery, we plug them in to recharge. We don't usually yell at our phone for running low on battery. Instead, we allow it to charge, and support it with a protective cover and perhaps a pretty case. We might forget to feed ourselves, but we are likely to remember to feed our phone.

Why are most of us likely to take such good care of our phones? Because we need them, we rely on them. If our phone breaks, we may not be able to communicate with the world, we may not be able to do our job, or connect with our friends, family, and colleagues. Similarly, we also need our bodies to be able to function and thus it makes sense to be able to plug into self-care and recharge our own batteries, just as we would a mobile phone.

I was born to Nigerian-born parents in the United States. I felt helpless and hopeless about the domestic abuse I witnessed growing up. Every time my dad would call my mom "stupid" or "ugly," I in turn asked myself that, because wasn't I a part of her? Was I those things too? Undergoing sexual assault didn't help either.

The biggest turning point was when I hurt my back. For the first time in my life, I focused on taking care of myself. I had to fight to make sure I got the care I deserved for myself, so I could heal.

I can't be a masked vigilante, but I can fight the stigma against mental illness and survivors of domestic violence and sexual assault. Currently, I run a blog called "The Living Resiliently Blog" where I discuss my own troubles with mental illness and trauma with domestic violence and sexual assault and how I try to rise above them.

Here are some things I learned from my struggles and triumphs:

- Don't beat yourself up for any childhood problem you faced. It was *not* your fault.
- Don't beat yourself up for any trauma you faced as an adult. It was *not* your fault.
- Your family may not support you in looking for mental health recovery. Do it for yourself.
- Your church may not support you taking meds. It's okay. Do it for yourself.
- And most of all: remember that you deserve to be happy!

—Chidi

"I always feel so guilty for taking a break, even when I am in pain," Divya says. "It doesn't help that my family criticizes me. They see me moving about and even smiling, so they assume that I am fine. I'm never fine. I'm always in pain. But I never thought it was okay to take a break."

"And how do you feel when you think about taking a break?" I ask her.

"Guilty. Like I don't deserve to take a break or that I *shouldn't* be taking breaks. I have work to do."

"If you did allow yourself to recharge, what would you want to do?"

Divya thinks about it. "I would go to the beach. By myself. I wouldn't have to take care of anything or anyone. I would just sit down in the sand and feel the breeze on my face... I haven't done that since... I don't even remember when."

"If you were to allow yourself to do that—to recharge on the beach in this way—how might you feel?"

Battery Charging: 90%

"I don't know why but I'm feeling really emotional right now," Divya says, smiling and sniffling at the same time.

"Self-compassion can be an emotional practice. When we receive kindness from ourselves or others, it might remind us of all the times we had not received it in the past. We might experience a flurry of emotions—gratitude, sadness, pain. All are perfectly understandable and to be expected.

"Have you ever heard the expression 'Sticks and stones will break my bones, but words will never hurt me'? This expression is nearly two hundred years old and is a fallacy. In fact, neuroscience studies find that whether we are verbally or physically abused or bullied, all of these occurrences are processed in the same regions of the brain—the ones that are associated with pain perception and processing."[53]

"I would definitely agree with that," Victoria says. "With all the physical abuse I went through, it was the emotional abuse that hurt so much more."

"I feel the same way," Tala says. "And you know what's weird? The part that hurts me the most is not even the physical or emotional abuse itself. It's that the other people in my life don't understand why it hurt me as much as it did then, and why I put up with it as long as I did."

"That's not weird at all. That makes perfect sense," I say. "When our loved ones invalidate our experiences, even without meaning to do so, they might be victim-blaming—putting the blame and the responsibility on the person who experienced the abuse instead of on the perpetrator."

"I tried to explain that to my boyfriend and my friends," Tala says. "They don't understand... Receiving messages from my mom early on that I am 'not attractive enough to keep a man's interest' made me extremely jealous and insecure. My college boyfriend used to call me 'crazy' whenever I would get jealous or ask him about whether he found anyone else attractive. The more I pushed, the more he pulled away. I would ask for reassurance and he would tell me that I am 'too needy' and needed to be more independent.

"At first, I thought that he was right. And then I found out that he cheated on me with four different women. I found conversations and pictures. I was heartbroken. I was so angry. When I confronted him, he turned it around on me, saying that if I wasn't so needy, if I didn't push him as much as I did, he wouldn't have done it.

"Somehow, I ended up feeling guilty. Somehow, I ended up being the one to apologize but I still wanted to leave. He promised that he wouldn't cheat on me anymore, and so I agreed to stay. A year and two more breakup attempts later, I ended up in the hospital. I seriously thought about killing myself. I was so confused and overwhelmed. I wasn't myself. I didn't know why I kept staying with him. I loved him and hated him at the same time. The entire relationship was so confusing, I couldn't understand if he was a bad guy or if I was 'the crazy one.' Looking back, I realize how unhealthy and toxic that relationship was. But what hurts even more is that when I told my current boyfriend about it, he said, 'Well, you should have just left him then.'

"We got into a huge fight about it. He still doesn't understand how much it hurts when he says that. He sometimes uses that word too, you know, 'crazy' or the other one, 'dramatic.' I keep asking him to stop but he won't listen. He just says that he's just 'stating the facts' and that I need to be less emotional. I feel like I'm fighting all the time. It's exhausting."

"You are so brave, Tala," Zaara says.

Tala looks up at her. "What do you mean?"

"You share your story with others. You fight for your feelings. What happened to you, the abuse, the cheating, the gaslighting, the invalidation, it's awful and you're still sharing your story. I just think that's so courageous of you. I'm terrified of being victim-blamed in the same way. I've seen it happen to many women in my community. Outside of this circle, I've never fully shared my story with anyone else."

"Well, if you ever want to talk more about it or if I can help you in any way, I'm here," Tala says.

"Me too," Isabella says.

"Me too."

Is there anything you would like to share with Zaara or Tala to support them? Please feel free to pull out your journal again and write down your thoughts, if you feel comfortable doing so.

The most rewarding part of my job is seeing people using their pain as the source of their inner wisdom, as a way to become compassionate and supportive toward themselves and others. All of you demonstrate how powerful compassion toward each other can be. And today, we are also going to be practicing *self-compassion.*

Self-compassion refers to providing the same kind of caring and nurturing response toward ourselves when we are suffering as we would toward others when they are suffering. The word *suffering* here means any kind of physical or emotional pain. This pain is not meant to be compared with the pain of others, meaning that we all have an equal right to be hurt by our pain. Other people's pain does not invalidate or take away our own right to be in pain and to seek support because of it. Some people may have different circumstances from us and different trauma histories, and we all have the same right to experience pain.

Self-compassion pioneer Dr. Kristin Neff defines self-compassion to include three main components: mindfulness, common humanity, and self-kindness.[54]

Mindfulness is a gentle, nonjudgmental way of observing the situation, as well as what we are feeling, sensing, and thinking. For example, mindfulness would mean noticing that we are starting to have a headache, or noticing that we are being triggered, feeling sad, angry, jealous, or overwhelmed. Mindfulness is the first step in self-compassion because we need to be able to recognize that we are going through a hard time in order to attend to and soothe our pain. A mindfulness practice might include a phrase such as: "This is happening right now. I am experiencing a difficult moment. I am feeling sadness, overwhelm, and anxiety."

Common humanity is the recognition that we are not alone in our experience, that many people around the world have and currently do experience the same things as we do. An example of a common humanity practice might include a phrase we might say to ourselves, such as: "I am not alone in this. Many people in this situation would feel the same way. My experience is normal and understandable."

Self-kindness is a subcomponent of self-compassion. It refers to the practice of asking ourselves what we need in a difficult moment and providing the same kind of loving and caring response toward ourselves as we would toward a loved one who is suffering. Dr. Neff reminds us that we practice self-compassion not to get rid of pain but *because* we are suffering.[55] Like wrapping a blanket around ourselves when we are sad, or like having a bowl of hot soup when we are sick, self-compassion is there to help soothe our pain, though it may not necessarily take it away.

"It seems so much easier to practice compassion for others than for ourselves," Tala says.

"Exactly," Victoria says. "I am much more patient with others, especially my pets, my patients, and my friends, than I am with myself."

"I also find that I am more patient with others than I am with myself," Tala says. "I often make excuses for others, even if they've mistreated me. I tend to let people off the hook for hurting me because I know that they have been hurt too. But it's becoming more and more challenging for me to be compassionate in this way."

"Being able to understand other people's perspectives and to be able to be compassionate toward others is the most incredible type of a superpower," I say. "And compassion by its definition is a direct response to suffering. In a way, compassion is a triage practice, which means that we need to tend to whoever is most injured in that moment first. Sometimes, that means that the person who is in most need of immediate compassion is you. Understanding other people's past wounds is a strength, and at the same time, it does not excuse their bad behavior in the present."

Tala nods. "I understand. It still feels like a weakness when it comes to me."

"Many people have been taught that self-compassion is a weakness," I say, "or that it's lazy or selfish, when in fact, self-compassion is essentially an investment into building our sense of resilience."

"But if I'm taking it easy on myself, wouldn't I just feel sorry for myself all the time and stop trying?" Lisa asks.

"That's a great question, Lisa," I say. "You just brought up two other practices, which are sometimes confused with self-compassion: *self-pity* and *self-indulgence*."

According to self-compassion research, self-pity refers to feeling alone in our pain, as opposed to self-compassion, which acknowledges that our pain is universal, calling for more connection with ourselves and others. In addition, whereas self-indulgence might lead to us overindulging in a substance or an activity, which might keep us away from doing what we care about, self-compassion is meant to allow us the break or the support that we need in order to be able to return to our core values and important actions.[56]

For example, a self-indulgent practice might be to take a week off work because we may not want to work on a particular issue, whereas a self-compassion practice would allow us to take the time off that we need *in order to be able* to return to our work. Finally, self-compassion research studies find that actually being overly harsh on ourselves will often lead to us losing the motivation to continue, especially when we encounter a setback. However, a self-compassion practice will allow us to continue gently motivating ourselves not to give up on a project or an idea that is important to us.

For example, a self-compassionate practice for burnout might be to say to ourselves:

> *I am feeling burned out, exhausted, and irritable. This is burnout. It's happening right now. Burnout is common and happens to a lot of people. Most other people would also be burned out in this situation. This project means a lot to me, so I am going to take a break for a few hours to rest my body and my mind. Then, I can return to it when I am more rested.*

There are different ways of practicing self-compassion. Taking a break is one of them. Let's think of some other ways of providing comfort and support for ourselves when we are experiencing physical or emotional pain. If it helps, think of how you might comfort a friend, a partner, a child, or a pet. For example, we might need a hug when we are having a bad day. We can ask for these things from others and we can also provide them for ourselves by placing our hands on our heart center, around our arms, or other parts of our body, such as our stomach or our face.

Zaara puts her hand on her heart. "This is nice. I can try this when I'm feeling overwhelmed. Or get a hug from my boyfriend."

"When I'm struggling, I think I just really need to spend a few minutes by myself, in silence, doing my breathing," Hannah says.

"I can relate to that," Divya says. "I also need to take a break to breathe and sit in silence, doing things slowly instead of forcing myself to finish everything all at once."

"When I'm having a rough day, I just want to cuddle up with my dogs," Victoria says.

"Music, painting, and meditating, I think that's what I need," Isabella says.

"I usually like to have a piece of chocolate or drink a hot cup of tea," Tala says.

Now it's your turn, if you're willing. In your journal, please write down what you may need when you are struggling or are feeling overwhelmed.

"That sounds really nice," Lisa says. "For me, it's reminding myself that I am allowed to take a break, and that I am allowed to do the things that I would encourage other people to do."

Self-compassion is a way of loving ourselves when we need love the most. This kind of love is fierce. Passionate. Bold. This kind of love is standing up to your external and your internal bullies. And it calls for the activation of your ultimate superpower: your sense of compassion.

Learning to be gently present with yourself and your own pain is not easy. Sometimes, years of abuse or criticism might teach us to use the same critical voice toward ourselves. The result is that we might beat ourselves up for suffering. We might feel bad for feeling bad, as opposed to having compassion toward our painful experience.

In learning to practice self-compassion, we can try writing a letter to our younger self in order to work on healing some of our old emotional wounds. If this exercise feels too overwhelming, you can always take a break from it and come back to it—no need to force yourself. Listen to your body and listen to your own needs. Doing so is already an important practice of self-compassion.

Self-compassion writing exercise

Think back to a moment in your life when you were a small child, perhaps a moment in which you felt scared, alone, sad, or in pain. See if you can remember what was going on and how you might have felt at that time. No need to write a lot of details in your journal, just a few sentences about what you may have been going through and what you may have been feeling at the time. If at any point you need a little break from this exercise, it is perfectly okay. Take as much time as you need. You can also download a PDF of this exercise with writing prompts at http://www.newharbinger.com/47520.

Now, see if you can see your younger self as a separate child, as a different child, perhaps as a little girl or a child of another gender. See if you can see the innocence in that child's eyes. Their pain, their longing to be loved and accepted. See if you can sense your own emotions, perhaps sadness, empathy toward that child, and your wish to soothe or comfort that child.

See if you can imagine approaching that child and perhaps sitting next to them. You know what they're going through, and you know what they need to hear. How might you comfort them? What might you say to them?

Take as much time as you need to think about what you might say to that child, the one who may be longing for your kindness and acceptance. See if you would be able to write them a letter of support and kindness, expressing what they might really need to hear. Feel free to take breaks and come back to this exercise if you need to.

If you are willing, next write about how this exercise affected you and how you felt about doing it.

"Me too. I feel the same way," Hannah says in response to you.

"During this practice, for some reason, I felt this very powerful sensation in my stomach," Lisa says. "Normally, I try to avoid feeling my stomach, because I've been trained that my stomach is bad. But this time, in seeing my younger self, in seeing that little girl, I felt a kind of fire in my stomach. Almost like a strength."

"That's fantastic, Lisa," I say. "Our stomach is actually one of the places of our strength, it is our core. In Japanese culture, the word *hara* means stomach, but it also means *vitality* and *courage.* Our gut is a place of our intuition, our feminine power. In some cultures, it is believed that our stomach might sometimes be big because it has to be. Because it stores our strength. So perhaps, instead of ignoring our stomach, we need to be doing exactly what you so wisely discovered, connecting with it, soothing it, caring for it, as we would for a child, and listening to it, as we would to a wise elder."

"I found the same to be true for my chest," Isabella says. "I've had a love-hate relationship with my breasts because of my cancer. But I realized today that all my love and my passion lives in my chest. I've thought about this for a while, and I've decided that I am going to get a survivor tattoo. My body is a work of art and I am going to celebrate it."

"That's wonderful, Isabella," I say, feeling my own eyes water. "We are meant to be celebrated, and what an amazing way to celebrate yourself."

> I've had to fight for every ounce of happiness I feel. I've resented it my whole life. The last five years I've begun to embrace it! I have to work twice as hard as others for less but it's okay because I'm a fighter. I was made for this. I'm stronger, more compassionate, thicker skinned, able to laugh easier. I'm a lover and determined woman. The key is to embrace the fight, not resent it. I'm a better person for it.
>
> —Jennifer

Whereas self-compassion refers to supporting yourself when you are suffering, loving-kindness encourages you to be kind to yourself even when you are not suffering but just because you are a human being who is worthy of love. The concepts of *loving-kindness* and *gratitude* teach us to celebrate ourselves, be kind to ourselves, and be grateful for the lovely moments in our lives. To be grateful for something may include *savoring and giving thanks.*

Savoring our experiences is like savoring a piece of chocolate or a sip of our favorite drink. For example, we might savor a hot cup of tea or coffee in the morning, noticing the way that the cup warms our hands, noticing its aroma, noticing its taste and the warmth of this beverage soothing our throat and chest as we drink it. We might then mindfully acknowledge that we feel grateful for that experience.

In addition, we might also be grateful for a particular person, pet, book, or movie that got us through a painful experience. Or we might be grateful to someone for an act of kindness they've taken toward us.

One way to practice gratitude is to keep a journal in which we can write one thing we're grateful for on a particular day. It could be something that occurred that day, or it could be a sweet moment or a memory of a past event. It helps if you write a few details to describe what you are grateful for, as opposed to just listing the event, because describing what we are grateful for in detail can activate our sensory centers and can allow us to be more connected with the experience of gratitude.

Another gratitude practice is to write a letter to a specific person to whom you are grateful for a particular action or a set of actions. This person could be a real living person, a deceased person, a celebrity, a historical figure, or a fictional character. Even if you never give them the letter, the process of writing it can be helpful.

Tala raises her hand. "What if I can't? My family tells me all the time that I should be grateful that I have them, that I had a roof over my head, and that I don't have the problems that other people have. But I don't feel grateful. I just feel angry when they say that."

"Exactly," I say to her. "You brought up a powerful point, Tala. Sometimes, people try to force us to feel gratitude and inadvertently might even shame us for not feeling grateful or for feeling upset. Of course, you would feel upset in that situation. Anyone would. What you are describing is called *gratitude shaming.*

"Gratitude shaming occurs when someone may try to shame us into gratitude. This often occurs when we may be struggling with an emotionally or physically painful experience, and a loved one may make a misguided attempt to make us feel better by reminding us about 'how good' we have it. They might say that we 'should be grateful' because 'at least it's not as bad as other people have it.' In fact, 'at least' hardly ever makes anyone feel better; it usually leaves us feeling ashamed, depressed, and alone."

"That makes sense to me," Divya says. "I've definitely experienced gratitude shaming too. I'm wondering, does this also apply to taking care of other people? I notice that although, of course, I am grateful for my family, I sometimes feel bitter toward taking care of them, especially when I am in pain."

"Thank you so much for bringing this up, Divya," I say. "Caretaker fatigue can often lead to burnout, which then can make us irritable and resentful. When taking care of others, we might sometimes need to triage too, meaning that we may need to assess who needs to be taken care of first."

In many cases, when we are the caretaker, we are the first person who needs compassion and support. Like a passenger on the plane using an oxygen mask, we need to ensure our own safety and well-being before assisting others. This allows us to have the strength and the resilience that we need to be Super-Women. This practice is not only okay, it is necessary to support ourselves, *so that* we can have the stamina to support others. Sometimes, this may mean setting boundaries with our loved ones and letting them know that we will help them in a little while, after we are done recharging.

Divya considers this for a few moments. "What you're saying makes a lot of sense. But I don't think this will work in my family. I don't think my husband will like me taking breaks and doing something before I take care of him and the children."

"He may not. What is the alternative?"

"Hmm. I guess, doing what I've been doing. I know. It's not sustainable. This... *self-compassion*... it's not easy."

I shake my head. "No. It's not. It may be the most challenging thing you do."

She takes a breath. "Okay. I will try it."

Superhero Training Steps: If you are willing, see if you can practice self-compassion, gratitude, and savoring. Take as much time as you need. No need to force yourself with this practice. Please give yourself the permission to do as much or as little of it as you feel comfortable doing. Simply answer these questions in your journal, or go to http://www.newharbinger.com/47520 to download a PDF of this exercise with writing prompts.

Mindfulness: Noticing a difficult situation

What is going on?

What do I notice about what I feel and what I think?

Common Humanity:

Can I remind myself that a lot of people in my situation would be going through the same thing?

Self-Kindness:

What do I need right now? What can help me get through this moment?

Savoring:

What is something you might observe right now that you might savor? A taste of a hot cup of tea or coffee? A warm blanket? A cool cloth? A plant? A picture or scenery around you? See if you can take a few moments to breathe and observe.

Write the name of a person, pet, or action you are grateful for once a day. This could be about something happening right now or about something that occurred in the past.

Write a letter to someone who inspired you or assisted you at a time when you were struggling. This could be a family member, partner, friend, teacher, deceased person, celebrity, or even a fictional character. If you are willing, please write them a letter of gratitude about how much their words or actions mean to you.

Chapter 8

Meeting Your Superheroes

Isabella is glowing with a smile. "I just wanted to say that I am so very grateful to all of you. Last time we met, I was really inspired by all your support. I ended up getting my survivor tattoo. I have hated my breasts for years, ever since my diagnosis, but this tattoo is my step toward emotional healing. My body is my canvas. It is my work of art and my chest is the heart of it."

Isabella stops for a moment, dabbing her eyes with a tissue. She then smiles. "And I just want to say, from the bottom of my heart, thank you. To all of you for supporting me through it."

Zaara raises her hand. "I wanted to thank all of you as well. I was really inspired by everyone's courage last session. So I decided to tell my best friend about the assault..." She takes a breath. "I wasn't sure how she would react. Outside of this group, she's the first person I've told my full story."

"That was a very courageous choice, Zaara," I tell her. "How did it go?"

"I cried when I started to tell her. She started crying too. Then she told me that she was also assaulted and never told anyone. She said she was scared of being judged and ostracized from the community. She said that me sharing my story made her feel safer to share hers."

"Wow. How did that feel?"

She smiles and sniffles at the same time. "Empowering. We held each other and cried. It's awful what happened to her and it's awful what happened to me. But I'm glad that I have someone to talk to about this and that we can both support each other through this."

"That's amazing," Isabella says. "I wish I had you to talk to when my first assault happened."

"I'm here now," Zaara says.

"That's true," Isabella replies. "I didn't even realize until just now that we are all here now. For each other, I mean. We can share and be each other's source of support."

"I want that to be true," Tala says. "But I might have to leave the group."

Everyone in the group is surprised. “What?” “Why?” “What’s going on?”

Tala looks down. Her lip is trembling. She wrings her hands. “I told my boyfriend last night. I told him that I needed compassion and support. I thought I practiced the skills we talked about. I used the ‘I language’ and I used the connection communication. And... I don’t know what I did wrong... He got so angry. We got into a big fight... I’m so confused.”

My hand is on my heart as I feel it pounding, feeling Tala’s pain and my own in response to hers. “I am so sorry, Tala. That must have been awful. Would you be willing to talk about what happened?”

She nods. “I’m just confused. I said that it would mean a lot to me if he would hold me and tell me that I am the only one he’s interested in.”

“That seems like a reasonable request. What happened next?”

“He got so angry. He started yelling at me and asking why I’m criticizing him. I tried telling him that I’m not criticizing, I just wanted his support. He said that it wasn’t what I said and stated that I said that he’s a terrible boyfriend. When I tried to tell him that I never said that, he started yelling at me that I did until I felt so confused that I ended up agreeing with him. I really don’t think I said that. I would never say that. But now I am not sure what I actually said. I was so exhausted at the end of that fight; I was willing to say anything to get him to calm down. I ended up apologizing for bringing it up. He asked why I brought it up in the first place, so I mentioned about the skills I’m learning in the group. He started demanding to know what we are talking about. I only shared my part of it, not anyone else’s private information. He got really angry again and said that this group is a waste of time and that it’s breaking us apart. He said I can’t come anymore...” She wipes the tears from her eyes. “I wasn’t sure what to do, so I snuck out of the house today and came in. I don’t know if I can come back.”

“That’s not okay,” Victoria says. “That sounds very manipulative and wrong to me.”

“Tala, I’m so sorry this happened to you,” I say. “I wasn’t there to observe what you went through but it sounds like there was a lot of aggression coming from your boyfriend. It also sounds like he might have twisted some of what you were saying to make you seem like the guilty party in the argument, and it is a possible example of *gaslighting*.”

"What's that?" Tala asks. "I keep hearing that term but I'm not sure what it means."

"Gaslighting is a form of emotional manipulation and abuse when a person purposely changes the story to confuse the other individual to make them doubt their own memory and perception. Gaslighting can include denial—for example, denial of the affair—and making the other person look like their perceptions are not accurate. As a result of gaslighting, an individual may be second-guessing themselves, might consistently feel inadequate, might not feel like themselves, might end up being the one to apologize even in situations in which the other person is at fault, and might have difficulty understanding the situation clearly."

"I've been through that in the past," Isabella says. "It was the worst experience of my life. I felt like I was losing my mind. When I finally got away, I realized that my ex was manipulating our every conversation to the point that I couldn't trust myself at all."

Tala thinks about it. "I don't know. I don't know what to do."

"Whatever you decide to do, Tala, the sanctuary will always be here for you and the sanctuary will always welcome you wherever you are, whenever you decide to come."

She nods. "Thank you. I don't know... but thank you. It helps to know that I can come back at any time if I need to."

"Of course, Tala."

"You know," Victoria shares, "I wasn't sure if I would be able to share this, but I think I need to. I've been in several abusive relationships and two of them turned very violent. I remember one specific day I really thought I was going to die."

"I'm so sorry," Tala says, holding Victoria's hand. "That's terrible. No one should have to go through that. How did you get through it?"

"The therapist that I was working with at the time helped me to put together a plan. She helped me to prepare a 'to-go bag'—you know, all the essentials. I had my documents, wallet with my ID and money, car keys, my phone, a phone charger, and a list of places I could go to—my friends, the nearest motel, and a shelter. My therapist also taught me to make sure that I always had my to-go bag near me and my car fully fueled, in case I needed to leave quickly. I also had a change of clothes in my trunk.

"Leaving was the scariest thing I've ever done. I questioned my decision for months before and for weeks after. But the more time passed, the more I realized the hold he had on me and how unsafe and unhealthy our relationship was. I managed to get away, and after that I helped a few of my friends to do the same. Hearing the way your boyfriend is treating you makes me worry about your safety. He sounds like he might be manipulative and aggressive."

Tala looks at her for a few moments without speaking. "Wow. Thank you for sharing your story. I...my boyfriend never hit me. He's grabbed me a few times and sometimes I get scared when he yells at me, but he never hit me." She sighs. "I don't know. Sometimes I think I'm being a 'drama queen' and making a big deal over nothing. Like, I think that I'm just exaggerating and maybe it's not that bad. But other times, I wonder why I'm staying with him. I love him. But we fight so much. I am scared to talk to him, and I feel like I'm walking on eggshells all the time."

"I remember that feeling," Lisa says. "One of my ex-boyfriends used to be like that. I was terrified of setting him off. If I said something he didn't like or tried to stand up for myself, he would turn it around on me. He would tell me that all of his friends told him to break up with me because I'm fat. I would cry and he would tell me that it was my fault, that I made him so mad that he had to yell at me, and I would end up apologizing. I found out later that all of his friends actually really liked me and never said anything bad about me. He was using my low self-esteem and those manipulations to keep me from leaving him. He never hit me either, but the emotional scars of that relationship still haunt me. That 'walking on eggshells' feeling you're talking about... I think that's a red flag."

Don't feel obligated, but if you are open to it, would you be willing to share something about your experience or offer some words of encouragement for Tala? If so, grab your journal and start writing.

"Thank you so much for that," Tala says. "That's really helpful to hear. I'm not sure that I'm ready to make any big decisions like that, but hearing all of you talk about your experiences is giving me a lot to think about."

"Tala," Hannah says, "if you ever need a place to stay, you can stay with me if you need to."

"Or me," Divya adds.

"Or me," Zaara says.

Tala smiles through the tears. "Thank you. Thank you so much."

I smile at all of you. My heart is warming at the way all of you are supporting one another. Like sisters. Like superheroes.

> I knew I wasn't what everyone said I was from the second my self-awareness kicked in when I was a toddler. I knew I wasn't a boy, and that I was a girl. I knew of bigotry and hatred toward femininity and people like me from an early age, so I suffered through life being what society demanded.
>
> It took me almost thirty years of my life to finally accept myself and make the steps toward being myself. I had given up on life and didn't see any reason at all for living. I had the strong urge to write about the character of Reina, and as I was writing I could hear her voice in my mind saying: "Why don't you listen to yourself for once? Stop pretending to be what others want and just be yourself, be the woman you were meant to be. You created me as a way to let a part of yourself live; well, here's your heart saying start living before you die."
>
> Her words set off an epiphany and I began the process of accepting myself and making the slow steps toward being myself.
>
> I can say now, be true to yourself. There are always risks but life is far too short to live with regret and oppression. Live before it's too late.
>
> —Reina

Today, we are going to be working on connecting with our sense of purpose. Your sense of purpose is your superhero quest. It is your heroic journey. The sense of purpose has to do with categories of actions, morals, and interactions that give us meaning. Such categories may include helping others, connecting with family and friends, romantic relationships, or creativity.

They may also include our interests, such as reading, gaming, cosplaying, watching TV shows or movies, or attending comic conventions, as well as spending time in nature, helping the environment, spirituality, and others. These categories of our sense of purpose are also known as our *core values* in acceptance and commitment therapy.[57]

Here are some common categories, which may be in line with our sense of purpose:

- Meaningful relationships and connections (family, friends, romantic relationships, and pets)
- Health, mindfulness, and self-care
- Helping others
- Travel
- Creativity
- Interests, passions, and hobbies
- Spirituality, religion, or atheism
- Culture and customs
- Learning, education
- Career (including your job and connections with your coworkers and, possibly, clients, students, and other consumers)
- Animal rights
- Environment
- Social justice or politics

Some of these categories may be important and relevant to you and some may not be. There also may be other interactions or connections that are not listed here. Feel free to write them in your journal.

Your sense of purpose is defined by *you*. This means that none of it is meant to be obligatory. These are the life directions that bring *you* meaning, even if other people (family, friends, or others) may feel otherwise. For example, your family may value some traditions and you may value others. This list is about what *you* value, not what people tell you to value.

"I am glad you made that distinction," Isabella says. "My family and I have different core values. They value traditional values and I value being true to myself, even if it is different from my family's customs. I think that my sense of purpose is to be genuine to myself and to promote self-love and self-acceptance in myself and others."

"Me too," Tala says. "My family still believes in traditional gender roles. But as I'm learning about self-compassion, I don't think that it is necessary for me or any of the other women in my family to work as hard as we do. I think that taking breaks, taking care of ourselves, and listening to our bodies is just as necessary as honoring our other responsibilities. I think my sense of purpose is to help other people understand that they have the right to be compassionate toward themselves, even if others do not agree with them."

"It's interesting that we are talking about our sense of purpose," Divya says. "I used to think that my purpose was to raise a family. And that part has not changed. But another part got added to it. Now I believe that my sense of purpose is also to be an architect. I believe that I can design buildings that can help people and help the environment too." Her eyes water as she continues. "I've never felt it as strongly as I do now. I am meant to do this. I want to see a building I designed and see it benefiting others. For a long time, I thought I had to wait to follow my dreams until my kids were older or until my pain went away. But now I see that I don't have to wait to live anymore. My life can start now."

"Wow, Divya," Lisa says. "You said the words I've been really needing to hear. I'll be honest, I always thought I had to wait. I thought I had to wait to lose weight before I could do anything. I thought I had to wait to date, to travel to Paris, to take dance classes. I would avoid asking the partners at my law firm to consider me to become a partner. I don't want to wait anymore either. I am not going to allow my weight to prevent me from living my life anymore."

"This!" Victoria says. "*This* is what I really needed right now. I don't want to wait either. I am ready. I am ready to follow my sense of purpose. I want to continue fighting for animal rights, as well as for everyone's rights to be loved and accepted for who they are. And you know what else? I am ready to start dating again. I realize that I deserve to be treated with respect and dignity and that I don't have to put up with being treated the way that I was before."

"You go, girl!" Hannah high-fives her with a smile. "I'm so inspired. I didn't realize until now that I've been waiting too. I've been waiting to connect with my sense of purpose: of being a mom. I love my family and I love my daughter. I was waiting for so long for my anxiety to go away before I could hold her, that I never realized that I could have anxiety *and* hold her anyway."

Is there anything you have been putting on hold?

Would you be willing to share something about your sense of purpose and your past experiences with it with the group? If yes, pull out your journal and write for as long as you need to.

Zaara smiles. "That is so empowering to hear! I am so glad you spoke up about this. I can definitely relate, and I am done hiding from my anxieties. Seeing how important it was for me to connect with my friend and how neither one of us had support to cope with the traumatic experiences we had, I realized that I found my calling. I want to help people who went through a traumatic experience. I want to teach individuals to find their own superhero voice in the time of their struggle. I am going to start looking at graduate programs and I want to use my pain and my experience to empower others."

"A part of your heroic journey is discovering your own superpowers. It seems that you have all begun to realize that you are superheroes already. You do not have to wait to come into your superpowers. You already have them. If you do not need to wait to be powerful enough, special enough, important enough—because you already are—what would you want to do right now?"

"I would want to open a safe place for survivors of sexual assault and other trauma and help them to learn skills to manage their experiences," Zaara says.

"Yes! I love that and would want to help," Victoria says. "I would also want to open my own animal clinic, a safe space for animals who are sick, or those who were abused or rejected. I would also want to start dating again."

Divya nods. "I would want to design a sanctuary like the one Zaara and Victoria mentioned. It would have a human and an animal sector, and it would also help the environment in its design."

"I would want to make partner in my firm and focus on human rights, especially the rights of people who have undergone assault and prejudice," Lisa says. "And I want to travel to Paris and take a dance class."

"Ooh, Paris sounds amazing!" Tala says. "I would love to travel too, and I would want to use self-compassion to help myself and others cope with their painful experiences."

"I would want to hold my baby close to me and spend time with her and my husband," Hannah says.

"I would want to paint a mural that represents healing and recovery," Isabella says. "I also want to support other people whose families disowned them, the way mine did."

Take a few moments to reflect about your own sense of purpose. If you're willing, write about your feelings in your journal.

Considering our own sense of purpose and taking steps in our heroic journey is not easy. Thankfully, we don't have to go through it alone. Some of us may have real-life mentors, such as certain family members or teachers, community leaders, and other people we know or may have known at some point in time, even if they are no longer living. These individuals may serve as our superhero role models for helping us to find the wisdom, the internal strength, and the encouragement we need to follow our heroic journey and face the obstacles, which will inevitably show up, as they do for everyone. In addition, our superhero role models can be celebrities, such as sports stars, music stars, writers, actors, bloggers, YouTubers, or historical figures. Finally, our role models can also include fictional characters, such as superheroes from comic books and movies, as well as characters from TV shows, movies, books, and video games, who can serve as a source of compassion and wisdom for us. Some of these characters can serve as surrogate family members or friends to us in a time of need.

Take a few moments to identify your personal hero. This is someone you see as a figure of ultimate wisdom and compassion.

If you cannot think of a personal hero, that's perfectly okay. See if you can think of a kind of hero you'd like to have or look up to. What kind of qualities would your hero have?

Now, take a few moments to imagine that you have some alone time with your hero. Your hero knows exactly what you have been through, what your origin story is, and how it has shaped you. Your hero also understands your wishes, your desires, and your sense of purpose. Your hero is kind, supportive, and encouraging, and knows exactly what to say to you and what you may really need to hear.

What would your hero say to you? (If it is too difficult to think of what your hero may say, no problem. It happens to a lot of people. Take a breath. You can always try this exercise at another time.) If you are willing, please take out your journal and write it out.

"Thank you so much for your willingness to share this," I say to you. "How did that feel?"

Take some more time, now, to write about how it felt to get all of that down in words. Hannah nods. "Thank you so much for sharing that. I actually wasn't sure if I would be able to share what came up for me, but hearing your story helped me share too." She sniffles. "My hero was my grandmother. She was wonderful. She always sought to help other people. She didn't work but she was always working, you know? She was almost like everyone's mom."

She sighs. "But my mom wasn't like that. She criticized me in every decision I made as a child and continues to do so as an adult. I remember feeling so tense and nervous every time she would come into my room. She would criticize the way I made my bed, the way I put away my toys, the way I did my hair. Everything. And then she would come up with terrible scenarios about what could happen if I didn't do things her way. She once told me that if I didn't put away my toys, my baby brother would trip on them and twist his neck. I cried for hours after she told me that. I actually imagined it happening. I was so scared of doing something to hurt someone else, that I guess I started developing obsessions. So, in this exercise, my grandmother sat me down and told me..." She sobs. "She told me that I'm a good girl and that I'm a good mom. And to trust myself and my abilities. It was *exactly* what I needed to hear. I want to do that so badly. And I am going to."

> I had an epiphany about my superpower. I wrote about my story in a FB group where we support each other in all kinds of ways.
>
> Last night, I got a big hug from someone who followed that trajectory of dipping into the unknown and coming out a little less afraid of the unknown. She thanked me and I thanked her. What a gift to see someone transform!
>
> Thank you for all you do to bring joy into the world.
>
> —Valerie

Isabella puts her hand on Hannah's shoulder to let her know that she has the group's support while Tala hands Hannah a tissue. A few moments later, Hannah nods and thanks all of you for your support.

"Thank you so much for sharing your story, Hannah," I say. "It shows how much sometimes our past history might affect us and how much our heroes can help and influence us."

In practicing honoring our sense of purpose, we are going to practice embodying our heroes in our daily life.

The following exercise was created and contributed by Lanaya Ethington (used with permission).

Embodying Your Superhero

Bring to mind an action that you do every day. It could be something like brushing your teeth, washing your face, making breakfast, taking a shower, etc. For this exercise, you may want to choose an action that you can do while you are sitting down. Or you may choose to stand up and do an action if you are able.

Get into a comfortable position that commands dignity and respect. I typically have my feet on the floor, my hands in my lap, my eyes gently closed, feeling my shoulders fall away from my ears.

Bring awareness to your breath.

To begin, I invite you to bring your present self to your daily activity. Your present self is just whatever is here right now. Whatever thoughts, emotions, or physical sensations you may be experiencing. If you feel comfortable, I invite you to go through the physical motions of a daily activity, from start to finish. So, if you are brushing your teeth, for example, go through the motions of opening the drawer with the toothpaste, uncapping the toothpaste, putting it on your toothbrush, raising the toothbrush to your mouth, and so on. There is no rush to this activity, and your pace during the exercise may be different than your pace during the day. When you reach the end of the daily activity, start again from the beginning, and keep doing so for the next minute or so.

Now, you can stop your activity, no matter where you are in the process, and come back to your present-moment stance. Now, I invite you to step into your "superhero self," whatever that means to you. It may be a version of yourself that has superhero qualities, it may be the embodiment of a specific character, it may be the augmentation of a characteristic you really admire. It could be superhero endurance, unending amounts of patience, or the ability to get up if you've been knocked down. As you embody your superhero self, I invite you to notice any change in your posture, any change in your facial expression, any change to your thoughts or emotions, any changes to your physical sensations.

I invite you now to begin again the physical movements of your daily activity, using the stance of your superhero self. Notice the difference of how it feels to move, in your body, using your superhero self. Notice the thoughts you experience, as you go about your daily activity from this stance. Notice the emotions that are present, as you engage in your activity.

You may slow your activity and let your hands drop and come to the here and now. Let's turn our attention back to the breath.

"How did that go?" I ask.

Hannah smiles. "I practiced holding Sarah the way I know my grandmother would have held her. I felt both gentle and very powerful in that moment. I've decided... I'm going to try it tonight!"

"That's wonderful, Hannah, I'm proud of you for your willingness to take a step on your heroic journey."

Superhero Training Step: If you are willing, see if you can practice connecting with your superhero role model during the next few days. See if you can ask them for mentorship with some of the tasks you are managing, no matter how easy or difficult they might be. In your journal, see if you can write down their words of wisdom and practice your superhero posture as you're completing these tasks.

Chapter 9

Becoming a Superhero IRL

The news of the horrific attack at two local mosques in New Zealand shook the world. We take a moment of silence for the people whose lives were so tragically taken in a place where they should have been safe.

Zaara is the first to speak. "I've been watching the news all morning, crying, praying. I am Muslim. My religion and my culture are very important to me. I was taught that love of humanity is the most important thing. I did not know the people who died, but I feel like they were my family. I feel that way whenever I hear about an act of senseless violence in any location. I just wish I could help. And I feel incredibly helpless. It's devastating."

"I know what that's like," Hannah says. "I felt the same way this morning, learning about the shooting in New Zealand, and I felt the same way learning about the shooting at the Pennsylvania synagogue, and the Florida yoga studio, and the countless schools that lose children due to shootings or suicide. My grandparents were in the Holocaust. And now, we see the increase of swastikas and anti-Semitic messages everywhere. It's devastating. I want to rush in there, wherever the disaster strikes. I want to do something. I want to help. And like you, Zaara, I also feel helpless and devastated."

I nod at the group, as we all breathe for a moment, holding our own grief. "At times when we either commit or witness an action that goes against our moral code, we may experience something called a *moral injury.* Moral injury can occur in active-duty service members, as well as first responders, especially if they are unable to save someone's life or prevent something bad from happening. Moral injury can also occur in civilians, especially when we learn about such tragic acts and may want to help but may be unable to help directly. Of course, such tragedies will affect us. How can they not? At moments like these, your heart hurts because it's supposed to. It is what it was designed to do. Our heart points to what we care about the most and, in creating this pain, it gears us up for action."

"Well, I am ready," Zaara says. "I am done being afraid. Every morning, I put on my headscarf. My headscarf is my supercape. It reminds me of my purpose—to honor my faith and to honor the people of this planet and to be a compassionate superhero. I am here to help others and I am ready for action."

Tala raises her hand. Her eyes are red. She is clutching her purse. "I left this morning... My boyfriend... I left him. I took my to-go bag, my valuables, I blocked his number, I disabled the GPS tracking on my phone, took my stuff, and left. I am so scared. Over the past week, I started realizing how destructive this relationship is. I realized that you were right: he used gaslighting and manipulation to hurt me. There's more. He would sometimes have sex with me in my sleep. I didn't realize until very recently that it was assault. I tried to tell him that I didn't want him to do that, and he said that if only we had more sex regularly, he wouldn't have to wait for me to fall asleep to do it... I don't want to go back. I'm scared that I might because I have before, but I do not want to."

"If you ever decide to press charges, let me know. I would be happy to represent you," Lisa says.

"Thank you," Tala says. "I just feel so... embarrassed."

"Tala, you have nothing to be embarrassed about," Victoria says. "Unless people are in this situation, they may not understand how difficult it is to leave an abusive relationship because the very will you need to leave has been taken from you. I get it. We all get it. It took me four times to leave one of my exes. It's not easy and we are all here for you. And if you'd like, you can stay with me as long as you need to while you figure things out."

Tala smiles. "Thank you. Thank you to all of you. Because of my experience here and because of my experience in this relationship, I have made a decision. I am going to become a social worker. I want to help people who are going through abuse and neglect. It's devastating to see how much other people might suffer. There are times when I feel overwhelmed by sadness and I feel helpless. But today, I see that when someone is kind to you when you are going through a hard time, it makes all the difference. I realize that the way you are supporting me, is how I want to support others. And I realize that I can make a difference. I am not helpless—rather, I help many people.

I may not be able to save everyone in the world, but I can help many people by being present with them during their time of need."

Zaara smiles. "You're right, Tala. We may not be able to save the world or undo all the horrors that we see, but we can be present for those who are suffering, and that can make all the difference. I have been watching stories of people all over the world, people of all backgrounds, grieving along with the Muslim community today. Seeing people from all over the world stand in solidarity eases my pain, and I know that this is something I can also do for others."

"Notice what's happening," I say. "Each one of you has been so moved by a tragic event that occurred either to you or to someone else that you are now gearing up for action. Your pain is your origin story and your action plan is your heroic quest to becoming your own superhero in real life, or IRL."

Being a superhero IRL means creating your own path toward becoming the kind of hero you want to be. It means considering the ways in which you would like to use your own superpowers, such as your kindness, compassion, intellect, as well as your experiences—both good and painful ones—along with your expertise and other skills to help others, and to create a meaningful impact in this world.

One way to do that is to imagine that there is a movie that is going to be made based on your story in the future. The main character of this movie is you, the hero with your origin story, someone who, much like some of your favorite heroes, not only overcomes their obstacles, but uses their experiences to help others. If there were such a movie made about you, what would it be about?

"Mine would be about a girl who underwent severe emotional abuse by her family and other forms of abuse by her partner and later decided to become a social worker to help people who experienced abuse as well," Tala says.

"Mine would be about a student who was sexually assaulted and was also bullied for her Muslim faith and then went into treating patients who experienced assault or injury," Zaara says.

"Mine would be about someone who experienced a lot of shaming and criticism from her mother and then developed a severe anxiety disorder but was able to learn to manage it over time," Hannah says.

"Mine would be about someone whose family rejected them because of their sexuality, but also about someone who helps others find a new sense of family through connection and art," Isabella says.

"Like Isabella, mine would be about someone whose family rejected them, about someone who has struggled being true to themselves because they fear rejection and about that person finding a connection with themselves and others through helping people and animals who have been mistreated," Victoria says.

If there were a book or a movie made about you, what would it be about? Find your journal and describe your movie.

"Wow, very powerful. Thank you for sharing," Lisa says. "Mine would be about a woman who was fat-shamed her entire life and who finally not only embraced herself but also became a lawyer and an advocate for people who experienced abuse or prejudice based on their gender, skin color, cultural background, sexual orientation, or weight."

Divya goes next. "Mine would be about a mother with postnatal depression and chronic pain who finds herself after becoming an architect and designing a sanctuary to help people and animals who experienced abuse."

"I'm actually really glad we are talking about this because I have something to show you," Divya says.

She takes out a rolled sheet of paper, the size of a poster, and unrolls it. We all circle around it to see the breathtaking design of a sanctuary. A ray of sunlight illuminates the trees around the scene. Sky-blue lake water is seen in the background of a lovely one-story building with green plants and vines all around it. Two small waterfalls run on the side of the building.

"I got inspired to finish my thesis project. This is a sanctuary for women who may need support, a safe space, like the one we were able to create for Tala today. And there's also a vet clinic at the back. There are solar panels on the roof and the water system would use recycled rain and lake water to sustain the clinic. I am submitting this design for evaluation and I would actually like to build this in the future. That would be my superhero IRL mission."

"Wow! That's fantastic, Divya," I say. "How does that feel?"

"Empowering." She smiles. "You know, for the longest time, my MS, my pain, and my depression made me feel 'weak' both mentally and physically. But I see now that I am strong. I am someone who is passionate about my work and about creating this project, even though there are days when I do not feel well enough to contribute to it. I realize that my pain, both physical and mental, is a part of my journey. It is also a part of many other people's journeys, and it is precisely why I know that I need to not only design but also build this sanctuary."

"If you build it, I would love to work there," Hannah says.

"Me too," Zaara says.

"I can make the mural for its wall," Isabella adds.

"I can help in the animal clinic," Victoria says.

"And I can help with your legal needs," Lisa says.

"These are phenomenal long-term goals. And they clearly come from your sense of purpose, which allows you to see the big picture—what it is all for. Sometimes, it also helps to set small short-term goals that are also in line with your sense of purpose, a part of your heroic movie journey. Are there any short-term goals you would like to set for yourselves today to get started on your superhero IRL adventure?"

"I think I would like to reach out to my family again," Isabella says. "I realize that there is a chance that they might reject me again, but I would like to try. Also, I would like to join an LGBTQIA support group in the community or, perhaps, to start one."

"I would like to join an LGBTQIA support group as well," Victoria says. "And, Isabella, if you start one, I would love to join. Also, there's a guy I've been messaging with and I would like to ask him out on a date."

"I love the idea of support groups!" Zaara says. "This one has been very helpful to me and, seeing how both my friend and I experienced assault, I would like to start a support group on my college campus for survivors of assault and prejudice."

Would you be willing to write out a couple of superhero steps that you might consider testing out this week? Writing down the steps you can take can make the process feel less daunting.

"Wow, that's very courageous of you," Lisa says to you. "I would like to ask the partners at my law firm to consider me to become a partner... And if they don't accept my offer, I am going to open my own firm, especially to help other survivors of abuse, prejudice, assault, and other types of mistreatment."

"I love that idea, very powerful," Hannah says. "I actually already took a big step yesterday. I actually held Sarah, my daughter, for over an hour last night."

There are cheers and applause at this news.

"That's amazing!"

"That's great!"

Hannah is smiling. "Thanks. It was very hard at first. My intrusive thoughts were still there. I reminded myself that the inverse of my fears are my core values and that I care about being a mother to Sarah. The worst of it was before I picked her up. Then, when I held her, I was very anxious at first. Then I started to cry. Not sad tears. Just overwhelmed. Happy and nervous at the same time. And then something released, and I felt lighter. I just held her in my arms and rocked her to sleep. My husband was actually very patient with me and very supportive. It felt like we are a family again.

"As for this week, I would like to try to set up an awareness group for new mothers at our local hospital. A lot of women may not realize how much their bodies change after they give birth and how much those changes can affect our mood, including anxiety and depression. I would like to volunteer to provide some education about how to identify signs of emotional distress and how to ask for help."

"That sounds amazing," Tala says. "In addition to applying to school to become a social worker, I would like to ask some of the teachers at my local schools to let me do a few seminars to help students learn about how to look out for signs of abuse and how to report it."

Divya speaks last. "For my short-term goals I would like to submit all my requirements for graduation and... this might sound silly... I would also like to go to a theme park with my family."

"That's not silly at all, Divya," I say. "These sound like wonderful goals."

"Thanks." She smiles. "Since my pain started getting worse, it's been harder for me to walk, especially in the heat. My kids keep pleading with me and my husband to take them to a theme park, and I kept saying that I couldn't go. After last session, I started looking into options and I realized that I could bring a scooter to a theme park and I could get around on the scooter. I probably won't go on most of the rides because that may be too much for my body, but I can be there with my family and I can still spend time with them."

"Wow, Divya, that's a wonderful way of creating a balance between your superhero steps and your self-compassion skills. By using the scooter and allowing yourself not to go on the rides that may stress your body, you are practicing self-compassion. And by going to the theme park with your family, you are working on becoming a superhero IRL. Well done."

The key to this practice of becoming a superhero IRL is to keep in mind the big picture—what this is all for. Not all goals will pan out the way you'd like. That's okay. Keep going. Sometimes, as you are working on one of your goals, you may feel overwhelmed or triggered. It is perfectly okay to take a break, rest, and then to get back to your superhero quest. These challenges are not going to be easy, but they are necessary. Remember: "No mud, no lotus." You are stronger than your struggles, and your vision, your experiences, and your mission are all important.

Superhero Training Step: If you are willing, see if you can write down a few superhero steps that you would be willing to test out this week. They don't have to be huge. Anything can make a difference. You could work on your craft, or reach out to a friend, or check on a loved one, or check on someone who might be going through a rough time. Write down in your journal whatever comes to mind. You are capable of anything. You are a Super-Woman.

Chapter 10

Your Superhero Story

In the beginning of our work together, we worked on creating an origin story. Your origin story is the very beginning of your heroic quest, and it nearly always begins with some kind of a painful or traumatic experience. However, research studies find that our traumatic experiences can make us more empathic and more resilient.[58] [59] Our traumatic origins, or pain, our suffering, are the beginning of our heroic journey, not the end point. The destination of the rest of our quest is up to us. Learning from our painful experiences allows us to observe what we care about the most, and we can utilize this pain as our greatest strength to help others who are also suffering.

> Frequently I am asked, "If there was one thing in your past you would change, what would it be?" Honestly though, the answer is nothing. To change one thing I have survived is to change the person I am today. I am happy with the person I am, and I strive to learn and grow on a daily basis, but in my opinion we do not grow by looking back; we grow by moving forward.
>
> —SLC

Sometimes, the most powerful step you can take is to share your own superhero story. Sharing your voice allows others to know that they are not alone and to learn how to take steps to manage their struggles as well. Your superhero story combines your origin story with your sense of purpose, your superhero steps, and you becoming a mentor toward yourself and others, written from a survivor's perspective.

Would you be willing to give it a try?

Zaara raises her hand. "If it's all right, I would like to go first. My origin story is that I was severely bullied for my Muslim faith. I experienced prejudice, which I now know was not my fault. I went through severe depression and even thought about suicide. I eventually made friends and started feeling better.

"In college, I was sexually assaulted by one of my classmates. I was terrified to tell anyone because sexual assault is not always understood in some Muslim communities. However, I ended up sharing my story with my best friend and she shared that the same thing had happened to her. From talking to her and from talking to all of you, I realized that many people go through what I went through and that the best way we can recover is by talking about what happened to us.

"In sharing my own story, I was able to help my friend. I was also able to share my story with my boyfriend and he was supportive, understanding, and kind. I am now starting a peer support group on my college campus for other survivors of assault, abuse, and prejudice. I am hopeful that my story will help others, and I intend to use my experience to help other survivors."

"Wow, that was beautiful," Isabella says. "Zaara, you have a beautiful soul and I am very grateful to know you. On my part, I too experienced sexual assault. I am also someone who has dealt with a lot of trauma, rejection, and invalidation. I have experienced rejection and criticism by my exes, and my family disowned me for being bisexual. I tried reaching out to them again a few days ago, but they said that they are not ready to have me in their lives.

"I have a long history of shaming myself for my differences. I have never fitted in, but I realized recently that I do not have to. I am my own person. I am a piece of art, and art is meant to be unique. I got my survivor's tattoo on my breasts, and rather than hating my body for failing me, I now look at it as my own canvas, full of possibilities. I attended an LGBTQ group last week with Victoria and feel more connected to myself, to all of you, and to everyone I've met there than I have ever felt before. I feel every emotion on the spectrum, and I see my emotions as colors, each one as important as the rest. And for the first time, I discovered new ones: hope and gratitude."

"Isabella, you'll always be family to me," Victoria says, "and if your own family doesn't see how special you are, I do. We are all here for one another. That's what I came to realize. For the longest time, I saw myself as 'less than,' especially when I didn't think I was passing as a woman. Now, I see that I am a woman. I am a part of the group, a sisterhood. And we are all in this together.

All of you, your courage, your stories, your incredible steps that you have taken, have taught me more than I've ever learned before in terms of love, compassion, and humanity. And you know what? Last night I went out on a date with a guy I've had a crush on for a long while. I was nervous as heck, but it was amazing and definitely worth the anxiety. I am proud of myself for my courage to ask him out, and I am proud of each and every one of you. I am a Super-Woman. We are Super-Women."

If and when you feel comfortable, feel free to write down your own superhero story in your journal. Please give yourself the permission to write as much or as little as you would like. At any point, if you need to take a breath or a break, give yourself the permission to do so. Take as much time as you need with this practice.

Lisa smiles at you. "I always love when you share. You have a very powerful story. It's truly inspiring. Thank you. For my part, I've spent too much of my life worrying about my appearance. It started with my mom's obsession with my weight, which eventually became my obsession. I nearly died from malnutrition, trying to starve myself. I held myself back from doing things that I wanted to do, and I realized that I don't have to wait to live my life. I just booked a trip to Paris! I fly out next month. I've always wanted to go but I used to think that I have to lose weight before I could travel there. I now know that my weight and my health are two different things and I can focus on my health without obsessing over the number on the scale.

"I am starting to advocate for myself and for others, and actually inquired about making partner at my law firm. After having a conversation with the partners at the firm, I realized that they actually respect me but that we have different core values. So, I've decided to open my own firm next year, focusing on helping people who have experienced assault, abuse, or prejudice, and advocating for patients' rights in medical settings. I'm going to spend this year working to prepare to open my firm, and my current bosses said that they would help me with this move.

"I am extremely grateful for all of you, and I have learned so much about myself and about what it means to be a woman. I even took my first ever dance class last night and I *loved* it! I feel invigorated and excited to be on this journey. Thank you all so much for being a part of it with me."

Hannah raises her hand. "I'd like to go next. First, I wanted to thank all of you. I agree with what the other women have said: your stories helped to move and inspire me as well. I spent most of my life struggling with OCD, which started after my grandmother died. My grandmother was my mentor, my compassionate figure, so when she passed away, I felt lost and scared. Because I was scared of something happening to other members of my family, I started trying to control my environment, which in a way, gave me a false sense of safety.

"My mother's own anxiety made my anxiety worse, and I think that she may have had similar worries to mine. As an adult, I often worry about many different things, but after my daughter was born, my anxiety morphed into what's called *harm OCD,* which means that I started having obsessive and intrusive thoughts about harming my daughter. I learned that this is a common subtype of OCD and that these thoughts are not dangerous—they just *feel* dangerous. I learned that my thoughts are indicative of what I care about the most—the well-being of my child. And with that, I was able to hold her last week, and every day since.

"I still have those intrusive thoughts, which get worse when I'm stressed or tired but get better over time as I breathe and stay with her. I am now able to spend more time with her and my husband, and I notice that I am starting to trust myself more. I realized that I am very good at threat assessment and am therefore very good in crisis situations. I realized that I am a warrior, a Super-Woman, just like all of you. And I am honored to stand side by side with such incredible women."

Divya smiles at Hannah. "Thank you for your beautiful heart, Hannah. I am so inspired by your courage. I don't know what it's like to have intrusive thoughts like that, but I know what it's like to feel like you are in your own mental prison. Between my miscarriages, my MS, my chronic pain, and my depression, I used to think that I would be unable to finish school. I used to think that I could not be a working mom, that I would be a bad mom or a bad wife if I wanted to work. But a few days ago, I graduated with my master's degree. My husband said that he is proud of me, and my daughters called me a *Super-Mom.*" She sniffles, smiling. "I realize that I can be whatever I want to be and that I can do it all. My family and I actually went to a theme park this weekend. I used the scooter, and it was great. I was able to stay in the shade, take breaks, and enjoy my time with my family. I can't remember the last time I felt so happy and so inspired. I am a Super-Mom. And we are Super-Women."

Tala smiles at all of you. "My origin story began in my childhood. My family didn't understand emotions and didn't create an environment to allow me to express mine. My mom was so heartbroken about my father leaving that she tried to protect me by telling me that men cheat and that women steal men. Her own way of trying to look out for me was not helpful and made me scared, insecure, and not trusting of myself or other women. It also led to me lacking confidence around men. I had several toxic relationships, the last one being the most challenging one because there were good times along with the bad. It made it very difficult for me to be able to leave and to be able to see how unhealthy it was.

"I just wanted to say, from the bottom of my heart, thank you, all of you, for helping me get through this breakup. It was one of the most difficult experiences I went through, and Victoria, you were right. When I was in it, it was hard to see how bad things were. Stepping away from it made it easier for me to see how unhealthy that relationship was. I am still healing and recovering.

"I have now moved in with my sister, and between attending this group, seeing my friends, and registering graduate school for social work, I feel like I am making progress. I also talked to the head teacher at the school where I used to go. They are already beginning to incorporate mental health education into the curriculum, so that all the students who take the mandatory health class receive a few modules on mental health. They allowed me to come in and speak about how to spot abuse, how to ask for help, and how to report assault. The first lecture went very well, and it was incredibly meaningful to me to have had that discussion with the students. I could see that they really needed it."

Sometimes, the most powerful story you can share is your own. Somewhere, there may be a person who could benefit from your own story because they could be going through the exact same experience, feeling alone, ashamed, and unsupported. Your story can allow them to amplify their own voice, can allow them to feel less alone, and can help them to learn ways to share their own pain in order to receive the support that they may need.

This journey is never ending, meaning that your call to superheroism is always there. There is always someone who can benefit from something that you can do or say. There is always something you can do to make this world a better place. And in the midst of greatest darkness is where the greatest heroes are forged. When you feel overwhelmed and hopeless, remember that you are not alone. Remember that there are other Super-Women out there, ready to answer your call.

To help you continue with your heroic journey, I have asked some of the most inspiring Super-Women out there to send a message of support, specifically for you. Here is what they had to say:

> I believe that the overcoming of obstacles, of any variety, tends to lead you to develop empathy, resilience, and quickness. It fosters humor. It rewards and nurtures intelligence. It tests, and thereby strengthens, a moral core. It gives you what others, with easier paths, can only achieve over a much longer period of time. I wish you hadn't had to face the obstacles. They weren't deserved. But you are strong, towering, and beautiful for having faced them.
>
> —Jane Espenson (writer for *Buffy the Vampire Slayer*, *Firefly*, and *Battlestar Galactica*)

> Our creative fires can't be put out completely, but negative forces can bring them down. Surround yourself with people who stoke your flames. The rest can go to hell.
>
> —Felicia Day (actress on *Supernatural, The Guild, The Magicians,* author of *You're Never Weird on the Internet (Almost)* and *Embrace Your Weird)*

The first step to recovery is the understanding that you were the abused. And that it's not a character flaw in you that led you to being the victim of someone else's bullying, projections, illness, or disease. It can happen to the best of us and the seemingly most successful of us "Super-Women." The pain is the same. By reaching out, you help to heal yourself and then the world. That's the real superpower we have.

—Ruth Connell (actress on *Supernatural,* artist, activist)

Never apologize to anyone for what you've been through. Think of what happened to you as acquiring another piece of armor. That jerk? Just got myself a new shield. Rejected? Brand new helmet. Got a full set? Then upgrade. Use your experiences to make you stronger, because you are stronger. You survived.

—Jenna Busch (founder, *Legion of Leia*)

Hurt people hurt people. If we carry the hurt that someone temporarily puts on us, we only keep it alive for them. When we free ourselves of their burden without pushing that pain onto others, we can break the cycle and begin to heal.

—Anne Wheaton (rescue pet advocate, and author of the children's book *Piggy and Pug*)

When we are bullied or abused, so often we allow it to invade our identity and contaminate our views of ourselves. Abuse is always about the fear inside of the abusers, who can give only what they have inside. Hurt people hurt people. And healed people heal people. You are able to make a solid difference in the world in a way that only people who have known pain can. And your healing will spread like wildfire. That's what they told me, and I didn't believe it. But it's true. You can be more powerful, for healing and justice, than you ever dreamed.

—Chase Masterson (actress on *Star Trek: Deep Space Nine* and co-founder of the Pop Culture Hero Coalition)

A wise person once told me about the diverse groups who come together to learn meditation: "There's always trauma in the room." I've learned that that is true. I've also learned that there is an incredible, innate capacity in the human spirit to heal, open, and transform.

—Sharon Salzberg (author of *Real Happiness* and *Loving-Kindness*)

It is challenging to hold loving, connected presence together with fierce, empowered truth because their energies feel so different. But we need to do so if we are going to effectively stand up to patriarchy, to racism, and to the people in power that are destroying our planet.

—Kristin Neff (psychologist and author of *Self-Compassion: Stop Beating Yourself Up and Leave Insecurity Behind*)

Whenever I feel lost, hopeless or just plain sad, I remember two things: 1) The only way out is through 2) Better not bitter. The first reminds me I will get to the other side, the second reminds me how I plan to live my life once I get there.

—Roxy Striar (host for *Screen Junkies* and *Afterbuzz TV*)

Look at the people around you—the ones in your family, the ones sitting on the subway, the ones taking your lunch order. We're trained to be positive, to not let anyone see what we've been through or are going through, but for every cheerful smile and seemingly perfect life, there's always someone who is struggling with something you can't see. There's always someone who shares your pain, your sadness, or your trauma. You might think you're alone, but the truth is, you never are—and you never will be.

—Andrea Towers (author of *Geek Girls Don't Cry*)

There is so much strength within a woman. You have the massive power to create a baby and give birth, straight up despite the pain, the tears, and the mess. You love your children and your loved ones fiercely. You would give your life for your child and fight to the bone if anyone gets between you and your loves. Fortitude is who you are! A badass. Own it, Empress!

—Emma Seppälä, Ph.D. (author of *The Happiness Track*)

As a female author and journalist, I am constantly bombarded with rejection, misogyny, and even death threats on a daily basis, just for writing about geeky movies and pop culture. But the way I stop trolls and bullies from getting me down is knowing that I am not alone, and that I am stronger for not allowing this kind of harassment to stop me from being myself. Find friends who love you just the way you are and offer emotional support when you need it—especially when you feel attacked just for sharing your creativity. Always know that as long as you love what you do and do your best at it, then you are living the best life.

– Bonnie Burton (author of *Girls Against Girls: Why We Are Mean to Each Other and How We Can Change* and *Crafting with Feminism*)

Remember that it's okay to not be okay sometimes. The road to recovery is long and constant. But it's beautiful and full of hope. Be kind to yourself.

—Sam Maggs (host on *Nerdist*, author of *The Fangirl's Guide to the Galaxy: A Handbook for Geek Girls*)

> I had a really hard time accepting that I had experienced trauma. It took me years to even accept that I was dealing with trauma, and years after that to start telling anyone in my life about it. To this day it's not something that's easy for me to talk about. I am very open about living with mental illness, but this is something I continue to play very close to the chest. But what I have come to accept is that there is no right way to process trauma. You are not less strong if you haven't been able to talk about it yet. You need to process things in your own time and in your own way. If that means, like me, you don't even say what happened out loud for years, you're still strong. I know I think you're still a superhero.
>
> —Jenny Jaffe (actor, writer, founder of Project UROK)

Should you ever feel stuck, remember:

- Take your time. It is okay to slow down, especially when you feel like you do not have enough time. The more we slow down, the better we can problem-solve and figure things out. See if you can break things up into smaller doable steps and start there. Start small. Small steps are the most powerful ones because they allow us the ability to gain momentum without running out of fuel.
- Ask yourself, "What do I need right now?" This is a gentle reminder to work on building your emotional safety and supporting yourself as you are continuing on your heroic journey.
- *Power-Ups.* See if you can allocate some time each week to reviewing some of the skills you learned here or elsewhere. Reviewing your skills, and also learning new ones, is a way of creating power-ups to help you advance in your heroic quest. Games such as *SuperBetter*[60] allow you to create such power-ups yourself and then level up when you succeed at completing them.[61]
- The measure of success is not how you feel, but your willingness to complete the task regardless of how you feel. For example, if you are

feeling anxious when you are giving a presentation, but you end up doing the presentation anyway, this would be a success.

- When setbacks happen, as they inevitably will, remind yourself that they are completely normal and see if you can reset your intention. Take a moment, rest, reset your intention, and take the next step.
- Celebrate yourself. You are a Super-Woman. You are a beautiful force of nature. You are fierce and powerful. You have already been through so much and your journey is only beginning. Your kindness, your courage, your experience may have already helped countless others who look up to you. You are a mentor. A hero. A role model. And your experiences give you the wisdom to help others.
- Honor your scars, physical and emotional. Your scars give you depth, value, and wisdom. They give you the knowledge to give back and share with the world. Own your scars. They make you shine.
- Keep going! You are already a superhero. Your actions matter. You make a difference, and your presence helps others more than you can ever fully know.

Remember that every moment is an opportunity to practice your superhero skills. Every painful experience, every exciting moment, every rejection, every success is your opportunity to help yourself and others. When you feel overwhelmed, it is always okay to retreat into your own sanctuary for a little bit—to breathe, to rest and recover, and then to come out like a phoenix rising from the ashes, to put on your superhero cape and continue to make a difference in this world.

Unlike some fairy tales, we know that everything is not meant to be "Happily ever after." Setbacks can and will happen. Triggers will happen. Disappointments and let-downs will happen. They are a part of the journey. There will be monsters of insecurity, the dragons of depression, and the demons of anxiety. They are obstacles to overcome, your opportunity to use your skills. Because you are a warrior. You are a Super-Woman.

Here is your graduation cape. You've earned it. Feel free to color it, personalize it. It is yours. Your cape may not always be visible, but you always have it.

You are a real-life superhero.
Thank you for being wonderful.

Afterword

Well, here we are. Well done. You've read the hero's training manual and taken the first steps toward being the mighty Super-Woman you are meant to be. There's nothing easy about this journey. As women, we are fighting an uphill battle. We suffer from anxiety, depression, and PTSD at double the rates of men. Many speculate that this discrepancy is simply an issue of poor description—that men express emotional difficulties in different ways, by acting out or using substances. But this fails to account for the social and cultural context of the patriarchal societies in which we live. If you look at the systemic oppression that still exists for straight, cis-gendered, white women, which is far worse for LGBTQ, trans*, and BIPOC women, a different hypothesis begins to emerge. Here are just some statistics:

- Women are paid less than men for doing the same jobs (Bishu and Alkadry 2017).
- Woman are less likely than men to be introduced by their professional titles (Files et al. 2017).
- Women encounter more road blocks to professional advancement than men (Joshi, Son, and Roh 2015).
- Women must be seen as likable in order to succeed, but the more they achieve, the less they are seen as likable (Heilman et al. 2004; Rudman and Glick 1999).
- In groups, women speak up less, are interrupted more, and have their input dismissed when men are in the room (Karpowitz, Mendelberg, and Shaker 2012).
- Women are seen as less desirable when they outperform men (Park, Young, and Eastwick 2015).

- Women are expected to take on more non-promotable tasks at work that have little visibility or impact on professional evaluation and advancement (Babcock et al. 2017).
- Women are punished more harshly than men for making mistakes, especially in traditionally male occupations (Brescoll, Dawson, and Uhlmann 2010).
- Women, especially black women, are punished for expressing anger, while men are rewarded (Brescoll and Uhlmann 2008).
- Women take on more of the family and domestic responsibilities, even when they work outside the home (Pew Research Center 2015).
- Women pay more for store products marketed as "for women" compared with identical products marketed toward men, a.k.a. "the pink tax" (De Blasio and Menin 2015).
- Women are bombarded with and negatively impacted by images of how they are expected to appear (white women must be thin with perky breasts and flawless-but-natural skin; women of color must be light-skinned with straightened hair) (Grabe, Ward, and Hyde 2008).
- One in three girls will be sexually abused before she turns eighteen, a rate that is double that of boys; one in four women will be sexually assaulted as an adult (Black et al. 2011; Finkelhor et al. 1990).

Is it any wonder that life can feel more challenging for us as women? That we suffer from anxiety, depression, and PTSD at higher rates than men? And yet, this is only half of the story. What we also know is that women truly are super. Not just because I say it's so or because Dr. Scarlet has been cheering us on throughout *Super-Women*, but because the *research* proves it. Here's what I mean:

- When we are physicians, our patients are less likely to die or be readmitted to the hospital (Tsugawa et al. 2017).
- When we are on leadership teams, corporate financial performance dramatically improves (Hunt, Layton, and Prince 2015).

- When we are involved in group decisions about land management, environmental conservation improves (Cook, Grillos, and Anderson 2019).
- We bring new and unique skills to professional boards, and these boards are more effective because of it (Daehyun and Starks 2016).
- When we participate in conflict prevention and resolution, peace agreements are less likely to fail (Paffenholz, Kew, and Wanis-St. John 2006) and more likely to endure (O'Reilly, Súilleabháin, and Paffenholz 2015).
- When we enter the political arena, the lives of women and mothers improve; we sponsor more bills and pass more laws that impact women's health and well-being (Swers 2005; Anzia and Berry 2011).

Just look at the way Angela Merkel and Jacinda Ardern have handled enormous national and international crises, and how the countries they serve have not only survived but thrived in ways male-led countries have failed to do so.

We created the #metoo, #timesup, and Black Lives Matter movements, for goodness' sake!

As Dr. Scarlet has taught us, we all have personal origin stories that contribute to our experiences of pain, and our social and cultural context is a big part of that. But our origin stories are only the beginning of our hero's quest. Neither our history nor our context need stop us from blossoming into the Super-Women we are meant to be. Our stories are our calls to action.

We are powerful and we can do tremendous things when we choose to step out of our old stories, out of our comfort zones, and into the connection and challenge arenas of our lives.

By learning to create emotional safety, connect and communicate bravely and effectively with others (especially other Super-Women!), let go of the struggle to avoid emotions and vulnerability, become dispassionate observers of the thoughts and narratives that limit us, and practice self-compassion, we can become superheroes IRL.

This is an ongoing journey. There is no arrival at the heroes' headquarters where the work is done. Even Captain Marvel has to practice to keep her powers sharp. You will stumble and make mistakes, as all humans and superheroes do. The key to your powers is choosing to get back up and make the next values-driven choice, and the next one after that.

As a little girl and teen my parents called me "tubby," "little tubbette," and "tubby, tubby, tubby, two by four." I have hated my body for as long as I can remember. I was sexually assaulted in college. I struggle with insomnia and anxiety. But these things do not define me. I am more than my body, my history, and my pain. I am a mother, a wife, a sister, a friend, a psychologist, an author, a podcaster, a speaker, and so much more. I use my abilities—and my vulnerability—to share psychology with the world so I can help others. I am fierce. I am mighty. This is my superhero narrative.

Remember and call upon your superhero narrative and show the world your magic.

—Jill A. Stoddard, PhD

Mental Health Resources

If you are having a mental health crisis:

Call (800) 273-8255 (available 24/7 free and confidential)

Text: 741741 (available 24/7 free and confidential)

If you or a loved one experienced sexual assault:

Call or message RAINN: (800) 656-4673 (available 24/7 free and confidential)

Website: https://www.rainn.org

For survivors of domestic violence:

Call (800) 799-7233

Website: https://www.thehotline.org

For information on how to stop child abuse:

Call (800) 422-4453

Website: https://www.childhelp.org/hotline/

To find a mental health professional in your area:

Type in your zip code on https://www.psychologytoday.com

Acknowledgments

None of this work would be possible if it weren't for these amazing superheroes:

My family: my mom, Illese Alexander, Sherry Alexander, and Hera Kitty.

My friends: Veronica Belitski, Harpreet Malla, Jenna Busch, Chase Masterson, Paxton Dolan, Sasha Arkhipov, and Hilary Graziola.

My mentors: Jill Stoddard, Michelle Becker, Ariel Lang, Carrie Rodgers, Amy Lansing, and Kristin Neff.

My superhero role models: YOU.

Women's allies: my incredible editor, Andrew McAleer, my grandfather, my partner, Dustin McGinnis, Phil Sharp, Shawn Johnson, Ryan Buresh, Billy San Juan, and Nigel Taylor.

As well as all the incredible contributors and supporters of this book: Aisling Leonard-Curtin, Amanda, Amanda Keats, Amy Shoup, Andrea Towers, Annabelle, Anne Wheaton, Ashley, Bonnie Burton, "Bubble Girl," Cassie Stossel, Chase Masterson, Chidi, Christy Jedigoddess, Clancy Drake, Courtney, Danielle, Desi Gomez, Ellen Winkler, Emma Seppälä, Erin Nicole, Felicia Day, Giselle Gos, Hannah, Irene, Jane Espenson, Jenna Busch, Jennifer, Jenny Jaffe, Kate Hibbert, Kristin Neff, Lanaya Ethington, Lily, Lora Innes, Lorran, Madison Davis, Maggie, Michele Waters, Rachael, Ragen Chastain, Rebecca Sheppard, Reina, Roxy Striar, Ruth Connell, Sam Maggs, Sharon Salzberg, SLC, Sophia, Tanya, Thesally, and Valerie.

Endnotes

1 Neff, K. & Germer, C. (2018). *The Mindful Self-Compassion Workbook: A Proven Way to Accept Yourself, Build Inner Strength, and Thrive*. New York, NY: Guilford Press.

2 ibid

3 Scarlet, J. (2016). *Superhero Therapy*. Oakland, CA: New Harbinger Publications.

4 Cohen, J. A., Deblinger, E., Mannarino, A. P., & Steer, R. A. (2004). A multisite, randomized controlled trial for children with sexual abuse-related PTSD symptoms. *Journal of the American Academy of Child & Adolescent Psychiatry*, *43*(4), 393–402.

5 Scarlet, J., Altmeyer, N., Knier, S., & Harpin, R. E. (2017). The effects of Compassion Cultivation Training (CCT) on health-care workers. *Clinical Psychologist*, 21(2), 116–124.

6 Sormaz, M., Murphy, C., Wang, H. T., Hymers, M., Karapanagiotidis, T., Poerio, G., Marguiles, D.S., Jefferies, E., & Smallwood, J. (2018). Default mode network can support the level of detail in experience during active task states. *Proceedings of the National Academy of Sciences*, 115(37), 9318–9323.

7 Fransson, P. (2005). Spontaneous low-frequency BOLD signal fluctuations: An fMRI investigation of the resting state default mode of brain function hypothesis. *Human Brain Mapping*, 26(1), 15–29.

8 Brown, G. (2018). Fatphobia101: Six tools to dismantle weight stigma. Retrieved from: https://thebodyisnotanapology.com/magazine/weight-stigma-101/

9 Chastain, R. (2019). Dances with fat. Retrieved from https://danceswithfat.wordpress.com/2013/04/01/what-to-say-at-the-doctors-office/

10 Lavie, C. J., De Schutter, A., & Milani, R. V. (2015). Healthy obese versus unhealthy lean: the obesity paradox. Nature Reviews *Endocrinology*, 11(1), 55–62.

11 Carbone, S., Lavie, C. J., & Arena, R. (2017). Obesity and heart failure: focus on the obesity paradox. In *Mayo Clinic Proceedings* (Vol. 92, No. 2, pp. 266–279). Elsevier.

12 Brown, B. (2015). *Daring Greatly: How the Courage to be Vulnerable Transforms the Way We Live, Love, Parent, and Lead*. New York, NY: Penguin.

13 ibid.

14 Germer, C. (2019). Shame and the wish to be loved. Retrieved from: https://centerformsc.org/shame-and-the-wish-to-be-loved/?ck_subscriber_id=302667495

15 Neff, K. & Germer, C. (2018). *The Mindful Self-Compassion Workbook: A Proven Way to Accept Yourself, Build Inner Strength, and Thrive*. New York, NY: Guilford Press.

16 Linehan, M. (2019). How to work with shame. Workshop presented at NICABM. https://www.nicabm.com/confirm/shame/?l=0

17 Brown, B. (2015). *Daring Greatly: How the Courage to be Vulnerable Transforms the Way We Live, Love, Parent, and Lead*. New York, NY: Penguin..

18 McGonigal, K. (2019). How to work with shame. Workshop presented at NICABM. https://www.nicabm.com/confirm/shame/?l=0

19 Brown, B. (2015). *Daring Greatly: How the Courage to be Vulnerable Transforms the Way We Live, Love, Parent, and Lead*. New York, NY: Penguin..

20 Coan, J. A., Schaefer, H. S., & Davidson, R. J. (2006). Lending a hand: Social regulation of the neural response to threat. *Psychological Science*, 17(12), 1032–1039.

21 Danner, D. D., Snowdon, D. A., & Friesen, W. V. (2001). Positive emotions in early life and longevity: findings from the nun study. *Journal of Personality and Social Psychology*, 80(5), 804–813.

22 Baker, B., Szalai, J. P., Paquette, M., & Tobe, S. (2003). Marital support, spousal contact and the course of mild hypertension. Journal of *Psychosomatic Research*, 55(3), 229–233.

23 Coyne, J. C., Rohrbaugh, M. J., Shoham, V., Sonnega, J. S., Nicklas, J. M., & Cranford, J. A. (2001). Prognostic importance of marital quality for survival of congestive heart failure. *The American Journal of Cardiology*, 88(5), 526–529.

24 Inverso, G., Mahal, B. A., Aizer, A. A., Donoff, R. B., Chau, N. G., & Haddad, R. I. (2015). Marital status and head and neck cancer outcomes. *Cancer*, 121(8).

25 Harlow, H. F., & Zimmermann, R. R. (1959). Affectional responses in the infant monkey. *Science*, 130(3373), 421–432.

26 Ainsworth, M. D. S. (1978). The Bowlby-Ainsworth attachment theory. *Behavioural and Brain Sciences*, *1*(3), 436–438.

27 Pietromonaco, P. R., & Beck, L. A. (2015). Attachment processes in adult romantic relationships. In M. Mikulincer, P. R. Shaver, J. A. Simpson, & J. F. Dovidio (Eds.), APA *Handbooks in Psychology. APA Handbook of Personality and Social Psychology, Vol. 3. Interpersonal Relations* (pp. 33–64). Washington, DC, US: American Psychological Association.

28 Shorey, H. S., & Snyder, C. R. (2006). The role of adult attachment styles in psychopathology and psychotherapy outcomes. *Review of General Psychology*, 10(1), 1–20.

29 Levine, A., & Heller, R. S. (2010). *Attached*. New York, NY: Tarcher Perigree.

30 ibid.

31 Levine, A., & Heller, R. S. (2011). Get attached. *Scientific American Mind*, 21(6), 22–29.

32 Levine, A., & Heller, R. S. (2010). *Attached*. New York, NY: Tarcher Perigree.

33 Levine, A., & Heller, R. S. (2011). Get attached. *Scientific American Mind*, 21(6), 22–29

34 Levine, A., & Heller, R. S. (2010). *Attached*. New York, NY: Tarcher Perigree.

35 Rezaei, M., & Ghazanfari, F. (2016). The role of childhood trauma, early maladaptive schemas, emotional schemas and experimental avoidance on depression: a structural equation modeling. *Psychiatry Research*, 246, 407–414.

36 Spertus, I. L., Yehuda, R., Wong, C. M., Halligan, S., & Seremetis, S. V. (2003). Childhood emotional abuse and neglect as predictors of psychological and physical symptoms in women presenting to a primary care practice. *Child Abuse & Neglect*, 27(11), 1247–1258.

37 Chugani, H. T., Behen, M. E., Muzik, O., Juhász, C., Nagy, F., & Chugani, D. C. (2001). Local brain functional activity following early deprivation: a study of postinstitutionalized Romanian orphans. *Neuroimage*, 14(6), 1290–1301.

38 Levine, A., & Heller, R. S. (2010). *Attached*. New York, NY: Tarcher Perigree.

39 Johnson, S. (2019). How to work with shame. Workshop presented at NICABM. https://www.nicabm.com/confirm/shame/?l=0

40 Chapman, G. (1995). *The Five Languages of Love*. Chicago: Northfield.

41 Fransson, P. (2005). Spontaneous low-frequency BOLD signal fluctuations: An fMRI investigation of the resting state default mode of brain function hypothesis. *Human Brain Mapping*, 26(1), 15–29.

42 ibid.

43 McCracken, L. M., & Morley, S. (2014). The psychological flexibility model: a basis for integration and progress in psychological approaches to chronic pain management. *The Journal of Pain*, 15(3), 221–234.

44 Melamed, S., Shirom, A., Toker, S., Berliner, S., & Shapira, I. (2006). Burnout and risk of cardiovascular disease: Evidence, possible causal paths, and promising research directions. *Psychological Bulletin*, 132(3), 327.

45 Ahola, K., Väänänen, A., Koskinen, A., Kouvonen, A., & Shirom, A. (2010). Burnout as a predictor of all-cause mortality among industrial employees: a 10-year prospective register-linkage study. *Journal of Psychosomatic Research*, *69*(1), 51–57.

46 Shirom, A., & Melamed, S. (2005). Does burnout affect physical health? A review of the evidence. *Research Companion to Organizational Health Psychology*, 599–622

47 Chen, K. Y., Yang, C. M., Lien, C. H., Chiou, H. Y., Lin, M. R., Chang, H. R., & Chiu, W. T. (2013). Burnout, job satisfaction, and medical malpractice among physicians. *International Journal of Medical Sciences*, 10(11), 1471–1478.

48 Ke, D. S. (2012). Overwork, stroke, and karoshi-death from overwork. *Acta Neurol Taiwan*, 21(2), 54–9.

49 Chen, K. Y., Yang, C. M., Lien, C. H., Chiou, H. Y., Lin, M. R., Chang, H. R., & Chiu, W. T. (2013). Burnout, job satisfaction, and medical malpractice among physicians. *International Journal of Medical Sciences*, 10(11), 1471–1478.

50 Iwasaki, K., Takahashi, M., & Nakata, A. (2006). Health problems due to long working hours in Japan: working hours, workers" compensation (Karoshi), and preventive measures. *Industrial Health*, *44*(4), 537–540.

51 Ke, D. S. (2012). Overwork, stroke, and karoshi-death from overwork. *Acta Neurol Taiwan*, 21(2), 54–9.

52 Ahola, K., Väänänen, A., Koskinen, A., Kouvonen, A., & Shirom, A. (2010). Burnout as a predictor of all-cause mortality among industrial employees: a 10-year prospective register-linkage study. *Journal of Psychosomatic Research*, *69*(1), 51–57.

53 Cacioppo, J. T., Visser, P. S., Pickett, C. L., & Berntson, G. G. (Eds.). (2006). *Social Neuroscience: People Thinking about Thinking People*. Cambridge, MA: MIT Press.

54 Neff, K. D. (2011a). Self-compassion, self-esteem, and well-being. *Social and Personality Psychology Compass*, 5(1), 1–12.

55 Neff, K. (2011b). *Self-Compassion: The Proven Power of Being Kind to Yourself.* New York, NY: William Morrow.

56 Neff, K. (2003). Self-compassion: an alternative conceptualization of a healthy attitude toward oneself. *Self and Identity*, 2(2), 85–101.

57 Hayes, S. C. (2005). *Get Out of Your Mind and Into Your Life: The New Acceptance and Commitment Therapy*. Oakland, CA: New Harbinger Publications.

58 Greenberg, D. M., Baron-Cohen, S., Rosenberg, N., Fonagy, P., & Rentfrow, P. J. (2018). Elevated empathy in adults following childhood trauma. *PLoS one*, 13(10), e0203886

59 McGonigal, J. (2015). *SuperBetter: The Power of Living Gamefully.* New York, NY: Penguin.

60 ibid.

61 Roepke, A. M., Jaffee, S. R., Riffle, O. M., McGonigal, J., Broome, R., & Maxwell, B. (2015). Randomized controlled trial of SuperBetter, a smartphone-based/internet-based self-help tool to reduce depressive symptoms. *Games for Health Journal*, 4(3), 235–246.

Janina Scarlet, PhD, is a licensed clinical psychologist, an award-winning author, and a full-time geek. A Ukrainian-born refugee, she survived Chernobyl radiation and persecution. Scarlet immigrated to the United States at the age of twelve with her family; and later, inspired by the X-Men, developed Superhero Therapy to help patients with anxiety, depression, and post-traumatic stress disorder (PTSD). She has been awarded the United Nations Association Eleanor Roosevelt Human Rights Award for her book, *Superhero Therapy.* Her other books include *Harry Potter Therapy; Therapy Quest;* and *Dark Agents, Book One.*

Foreword writer **Chase Masterson** is a guest star on The CW Network's *The Flash,* which won the E! People's Choice Award for "Favorite New TV Drama." Her upcoming and recent feature film work includes *Robotech, The Search for Simon, Yesterday Was a Lie, The Inspector Chronicles,* and *R.U.R.*

Afterword writer **Jill A. Stoddard, PhD,** is a clinical psychologist and the director of The Center for Stress and Anxiety Management in San Diego, CA. She is an award-winning teacher, recognized acceptance and commitment therapy (ACT) trainer, and coauthor of *The Big Book of ACT Metaphors.*